M000084006

Origami Book
For Kids

Lizeth Smith

© **Copyright - All rights reserved.**

The content contained within this book may not be reproduced, duplicated or transmitted without direct written permission from the author or the publisher. Under no circumstances will any blame or legal responsibility be held against the publisher, or author, for any damages, reparation, or monetary loss due to the information contained within this book, either directly or indirectly.

Legal Notice
This book is copyright protected. It is only for personal use. You cannot amend, distribute, sell, use, quote or paraphrase any part, or the content within this book, without the consent of the author or publisher.

Disclaimer Notice
Please note the information contained within this document is for educational and entertainment purposes only. All effort has been executed to present accurate, up to date, reliable, complete information. No warranties of any kind are declared or implied. Readers acknowledge that the author is not engaged in the rendering of legal, financial, medical or professional advice. The content within this book has been derived from various sources. Please consult a licensed professional before attempting any techniques outlined in this book. By reading this document, the reader agrees that under no circumstances is the author responsible for any losses, direct or indirect, that are incurred as a result of the use of the information contained within this document, including, but not limited to, errors, omissions, or inaccuracies.

Curious About a Better Origami Experience?

Scan our QR Code Now and Open the Door to Seamless Creativity with your Newly Acquired Origami Book

SYMBOLS

Lines

──────── **Edge line:** Shows the paper edge.

············ **Creased line:** Fold line from previous step.

– – – – – **Valley fold line:** Fold when paper edge is facing to the bottom.

–·–·–·– **Mountain fold line:** Fold when paper edge is facing to the top.

················ **Imaginary line:** Shows the paper position after the step is done.

Arrows

Direction arrow: Direction to which paper will be folded.

Fold and unfold arrow: Only creased line needs to be done.

Turn over arrow: Model should be turned over for further steps.

Squash arrow: Shows that the paper has to be pushed down.

Rotation arrow: Shows the direction to which model should be rotated.

FOLDS

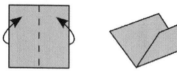

Valley Fold

Folding the sides up while making the fold edge go down.
Paper forms figure similar to the valley.

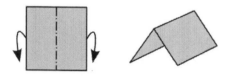

Mountain Fold

Folding the sides down while making the fold edge go up.
Paper forms figure similar to mountain.

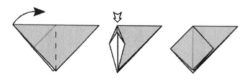

Squash Fold

Fold containing two steps. First the corner is folded vertically up and then it is pushed down using already precreased lines.

MODEL OVERVIEW

HEART

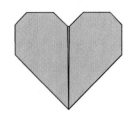
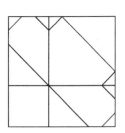

1 Start with the white side up.

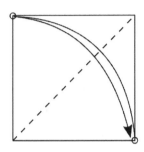

2 Fold and unfold in half diagonally.

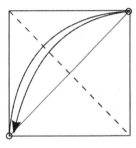

3 Fold and unfold in the half to the other direction.

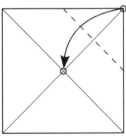

4 Fold the corner to the center point.

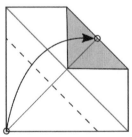

5 Fold the corner to the top middle point.

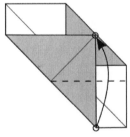

6 Fold the corner to the top middle point.

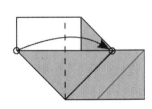

7 Fold the other corner accordingly.

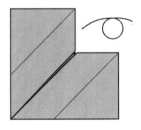

8 Turn the model over.

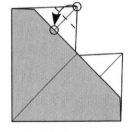

9 Fold the corner to the marked point.

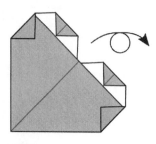

10 Fold the other corner accordingly.

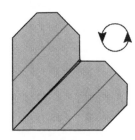

11 Fold corner according to the marked point.

12 Fold the other corner accordingly.

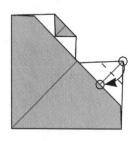

13 Turn the model over.

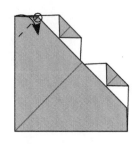

14 Rotate the model to the left.

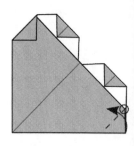

15 Finished Heart!

SWAN

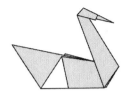

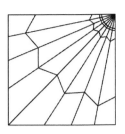

1 Start with the white side up.

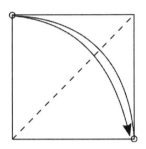

2 Fold and unfold in half diagonally.

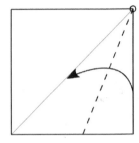

3 Fold the side to the diagonal line.

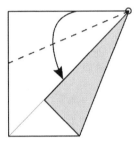

4 Fold the other side to the diagonal line.

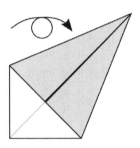

5 Turn the model over.

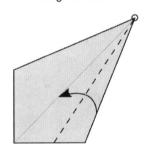

6 Fold the side to the diagonal line.

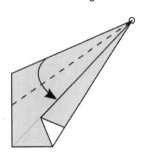

7 Fold the other side to the diagonal line.

8 Fold the top corner to the bottom one.

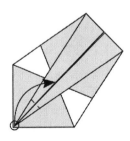

9 Fold the corner up.

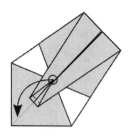 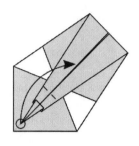 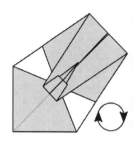

10 Fold the corner down.

11 Fold the corner up to form the head.

12 Rotate the model.

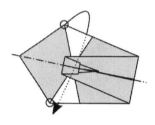 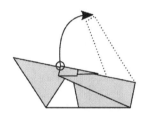 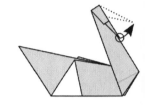

13 Fold the model in half behind.

14 Lift the neck and head up.

15 Lift the head up.

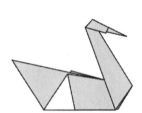

16 Finished Swan!

FOX

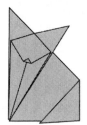
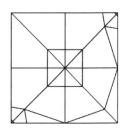

1 Start with the white side up.

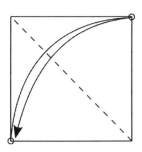

2 Fold and unfold in half diagonally.

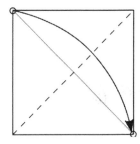

3 Fold diagonally in half to the other direction.

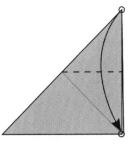

4 Fold the corner down to the bottom point.

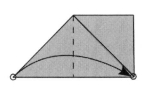

5 Fold the other corner to the same point.

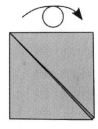

6 Turn the model over.

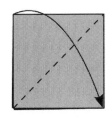

7 Fold the model diagonally in half.

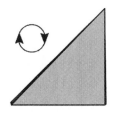

8 Rotate the model.

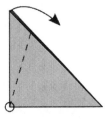

9 Fold through all the layers to the right.

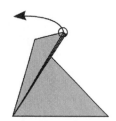

10 Unfold the top layer back to the previous position.

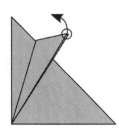

11 Fold the top layer perpendicularly up.

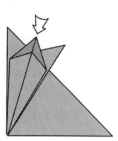

12 Squash fold down b separating layers to sides and pushing down the top part.

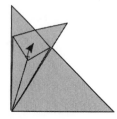

13 Fold the tip through the both layers up.

14 Fold the corner to the left.

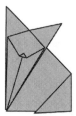

15 Finished Fox!

WHALE

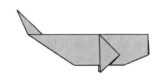

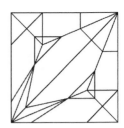

1 Start with the white side up.

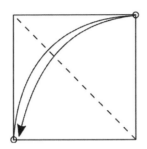

2 Fold and unfold in half diagonally.

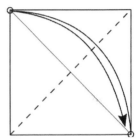

3 Fold and unfold diagonally in half to the other direction.

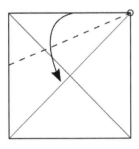

4 Fold the top edge to the center line.

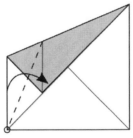

5 Fold the edge to the center line.

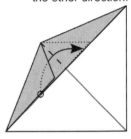

6 Take out the hidden corner to the top.

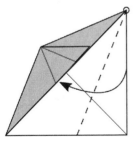

7 Fold the right edge to the center line.

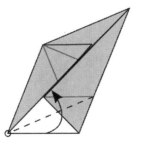

8 Fold the bottom edge to the center line.

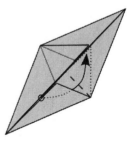

9 Take out the hidden corner to the top.

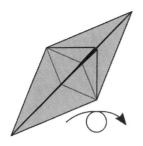

10 Turn the model over.

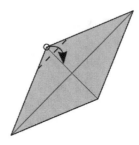

11 Fold the corner on the center line.

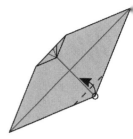

12 Fold the opposite corner on the center line.

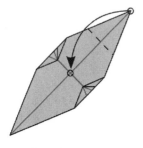

13 Fold the top corner to the center point.

14 Fold the model in half.

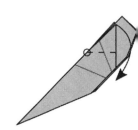

15 Fold the corner down according to the marked point.

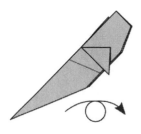

16 Turn the model over.

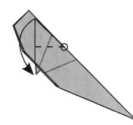

17 Fold the corner down according to the marked point.

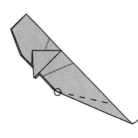

18 Fold the corner up according to the marked point.

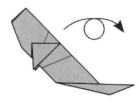

19 Turn the model over.

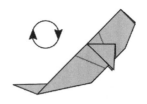

20 Rotate the model.

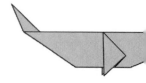

21 Finished Whale!

DUCK

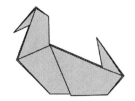

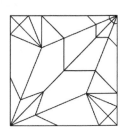

1 Start with the white side up.

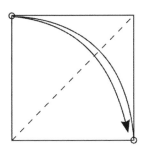

2 Fold and unfold in half diagonally.

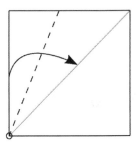

3 Fold the left edge to the center line.

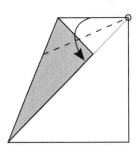

4 Fold the top edge to the center line.

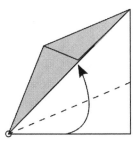

5 Fold the bottom edge to the center line.

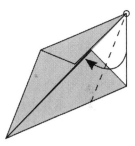

6 Fold the right edge to the center line.

7 Fold and unfold diagonally in half.

8 Turn the model over.

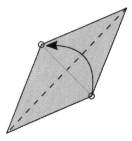

9 Fold the model in half to the top point.

17

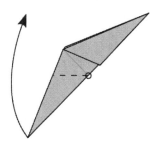

10 Fold the corner up according to the marked point.

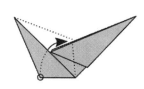

11 Take out the hidden corner to the right.

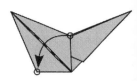

12 Fold the corner to the left.

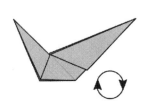

13 Rotate the model.

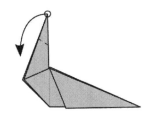

14 Fold the corner down.

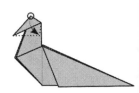

15 Take out the hidden corner down.

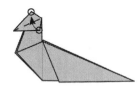

16 Fold the corner up.

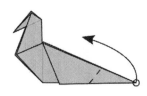

17 Fold the marked corner.

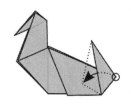

18 Take out the hidden corner to the left.

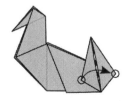

19 Fold the corner to the right.

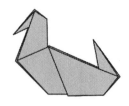

20 Finished Duck!

SAILBOAT

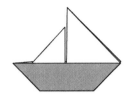 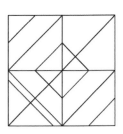

1 Start with the white side up.

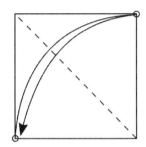

2 Fold and unfold in half diagonally.

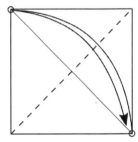

3 Fold and unfold diagonally in half to the other direction.

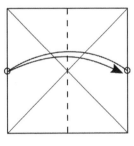

4 Fold and unfold vertically in half.

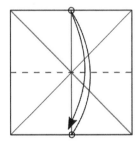

5 Fold and unfold horizontally in half.

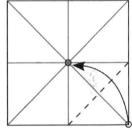

6 Fold the bottom right corner to the center point.

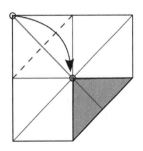

7 Fold the top left corner to the center point.

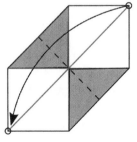

8 Fold the top right corner to the bottom left corner.

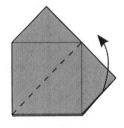

9 Fold the left edge vertically up.

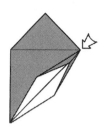 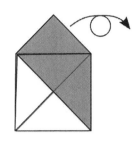 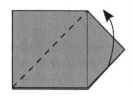

10 Squash fold the edge down to make the model flat.

11 Turn the model over.

12 Fold the left edge vertically up.

 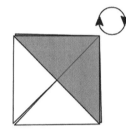 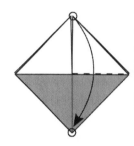

13 Squash fold the edge down to make the model flat.

14 Rotate the model.

15 Fold the top left corner to the bottom point.

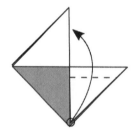 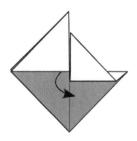 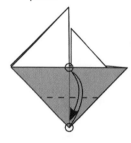

16 Fold the corner up.

17 Bring the paper layer from behind to the front.

18 Fold and unfold the bottom corner to the center point.

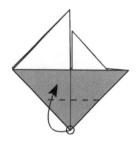  

19 Fold the bottom corner vertically up.

20 Turn the model over.

21 Finished Sailboat!

PARROT

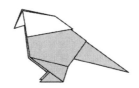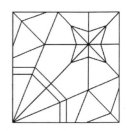

1 Start with the white side up.

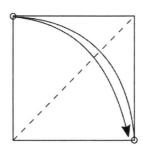

2 Fold and unfold in half diagonally.

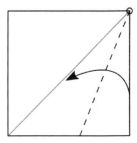

3 Fold the left edge to the center line.

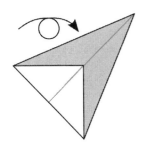

4 Fold the top edge to the center line.

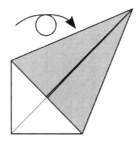

5 Turn the model over.

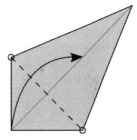

6 Fold the corner up according to the marked points.

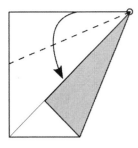

7 Turn the model over.

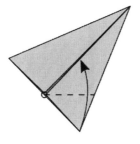

8 Fold the corner to the center line according to the marked point.

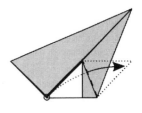

9 Take out the hidden corner to the right.

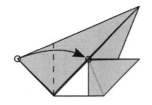 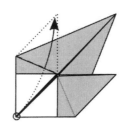 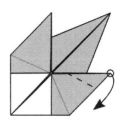

10 Fold the corner to the marked point.

11 Take out the hidden corner to the top.

12 Fold the corner dow

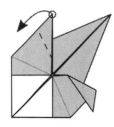 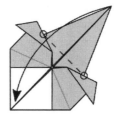 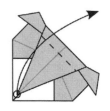

13 Fold the opposite corner symmetrically down.

14 Fold the corner down according to the marked points.

15 Fold the corner up.

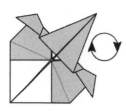 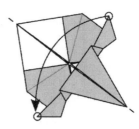 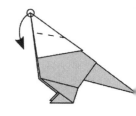

16 Rotate the model.

17 Bring the paper layer from behind to the front.

18 Fold and unfold the bottom corner to the center point.

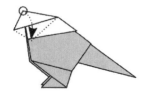  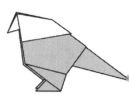

19 Take out the hidden corner to the bottom.

20 Fold the corner to the top point.

21 Finished Parrot!

22

LION

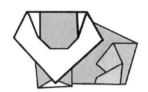

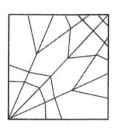

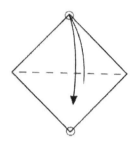

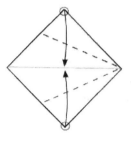

1 Start with the white side up.

2 Fold and unfold in half diagonally.

3 Fold the corners to the center.

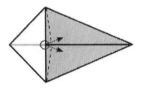

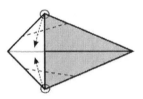

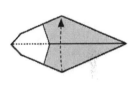

4 Fold the layers inside in the dotted lines.

5 Fold back in the dotted lines.

6 Fold in half.

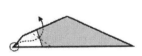

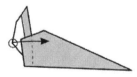

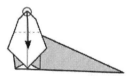

7 Pocket fold in the dotted lines.

8 Open the front layer to the right in the dotted lines.

9 Fold to the marked point to form the head.

 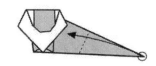 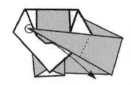

10 Fold back in the dotted line.

11 Fold to the left in the dotted line.

12 Fold diagonally down

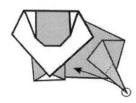 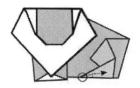 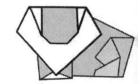

13 Fold to the marked point.

14 Pocket fold inside in the dotted line.

15 Finished Lion!

CROW

 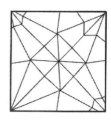

1 Start with the white side up.

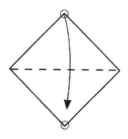

2 Fold in half.

3 Fold the model to the marked point.

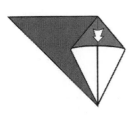

4 Squash fold the front layer.

5 Turn the model over.

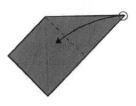

6 Squash fold the other side.

7 Fold and unfold the left, right and top corners to the center.

8 Lift the bottom corner up.

9 Squash fold the left and right sides.

25

10 Turn the model over.

11 Lift the bottom corner up.

12 Pocket fold bottom right and left corner in the dotted lines.

13 Fold the front layer down.

14 Fold the marked point down in the dotted line.

15 Fold in half.

16 Pocket fold to form the head.

17 Finished Crow!

MOUSE

 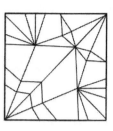

1 Start with the white side up.

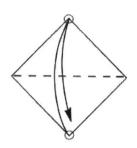

2 Fold and unfold in the half diagonally.

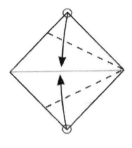

3 Fold the corners to the center.

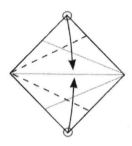

4 Fold in the dotted lines.

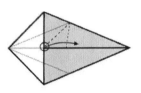

5 Fold down in the dotted lines creating a pocket.

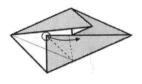

6 Fold the other side.

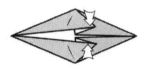

7 Flatten the pockets.

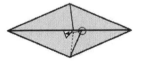

8 Mountain fold the flap behind.

9 Fold the other flap accordingly.

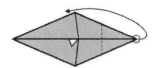 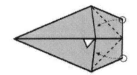 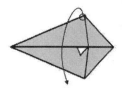

10 Fold the tip behind.

11 Fold back in the dotted lines.

12 Fold in half.

 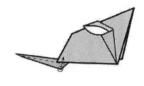 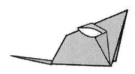

13 Fold the ears back opening the pockets.

14 Open the pockets to form the ears.

15 Pocket fold inside in the dotted lines.

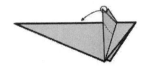  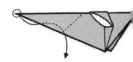

16 Pocket fold to form a tail.

17 Fold the flaps inside.

18 Finished Mouse!

28

SPARROW

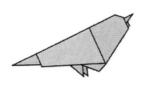

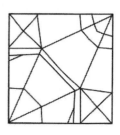

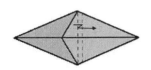
1 Start with the white side up.

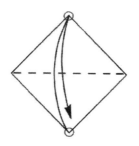
2 Fold and unfold in the half diagonally.

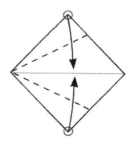
3 Fold the corners to the center.

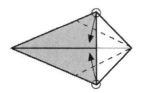
4 Fold in the dotted lines.

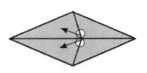
5 Open the pockets moving the corners to the marked points.

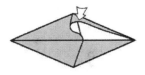
6 Flatten the pockets.

7 Step fold in the dotted lines.

8 Fold forward.

9 Fold the both sides in the dotted lines.

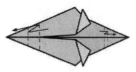 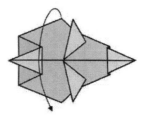

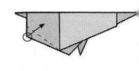

10 Step fold the both sides.

11 Fold in half.

12 Fold both sides inside.

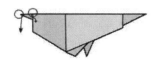

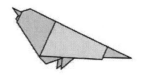

13 Pull down the beak and pocket fold inside the upper point on the head.

14 Finished Sparrow!

CHICKEN

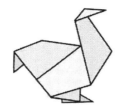

1 Start with the white side up.

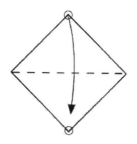

2 Fold and unfold in the half diagonally.

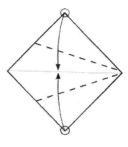

3 Fold the model to the marked point.

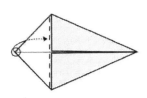

4 Fold back in the dotted lines.

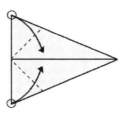

5 Fold in the dotted lines.

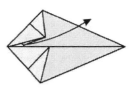

6 Pull out the pocket.

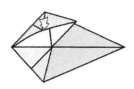

7 Squash fold the pocket.

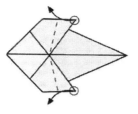

8 Fold in the dotted lines.

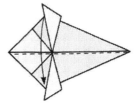

9 Fold in half.

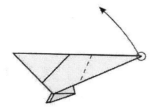 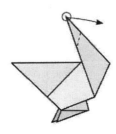 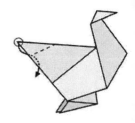

10 Pocket fold in the dotted lines.

11 Pocket fold the heads in the dotted lines.

12 Pocket fold the tail the dotted lines.

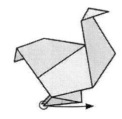 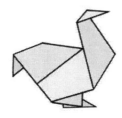

13 Fold in the dotted lines.

14 Finished Chicken!

CAMEL

 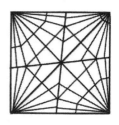

1 Start with the white side up.

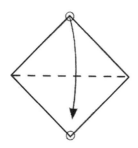

2 Fold in half.

3 Fold the model to the marked point.

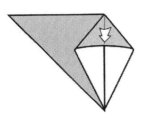

4 Squash fold the front layer.

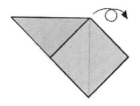

5 Turn the model over.

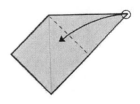

6 Squash fold the other side.

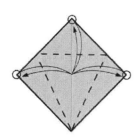

7 Fold and unfold the left, right and top corners to the center.

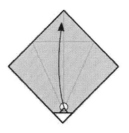

8 Lift the bottom corner up.

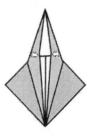

9 Squash fold the left and right sides.

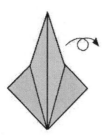 **10** Turn the model over.

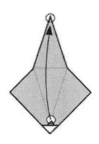 **11** Lift the bottom corner up.

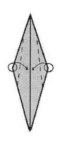 **12** Fold the corners to the center.

 **13** Fold the bottom corners diagonally up turning them over.

 **14** Fold the right corner down doing an insert fold.

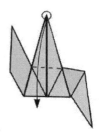 **15** Fold the corners down to form the fro legs.

 **16** Squash fold separating the layers and pushing down the top.

 **17** Fold the corner inside.

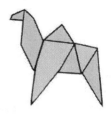 **18** Finished Camel!

RABBIT

 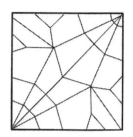

1 Start with the colored side up.

2 Fold and unfold in the half diagonally.

3 Fold the model to the marked point.

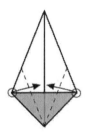

4 Fold the corners to the center.

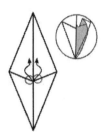

5 Open the pockets and squash fold according to the image.

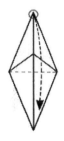

6 Fold back in the dotted lines.

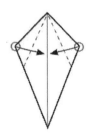

7 Fold the corners to the center.

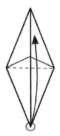

8 Fold up in the dotted lines.

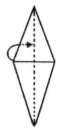

9 Fold in half.

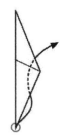 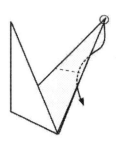 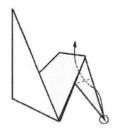

10 Pocket fold to the marked point.

11 Pocket fold down in the dotted line.

12 Pocket fold to the marked point.

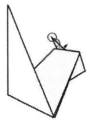 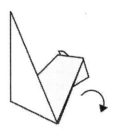 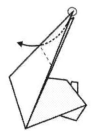

13 Fold inside.

14 Rotate the model.

15 Pocket fold to form the head.

16 Fold inside in the dotted line.

17 Open the pockets to form the ears.

18 Finished Rabbit!

SEA HORSE

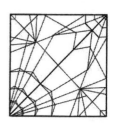

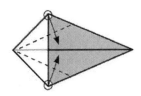

1 Start with the white side up.

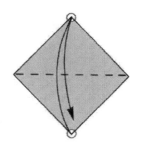

2 Fold and unfold in the half diagonally.

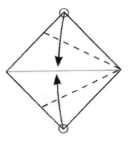

3 Fold the corners to the center.

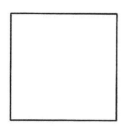

4 Fold in the dotted lines.

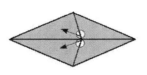

5 Open the pockets moving the corners to the marked point.

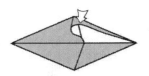

6 Flatten the pockets.

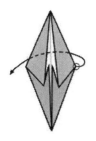

7 Fold in half.

8 Fold the flaps in the dotted lines.

9 Fold inside.

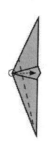 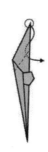 

10 Fold the both layers inside.

11 Pocket fold in the dotted line.

12 Pocket fold forward.

13 Fold inside.

14 Do a step fold.

15 Step fold in the dotted lines.

16 Finished Sea Horse!

CAT

 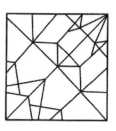

1 Start with the white side up.

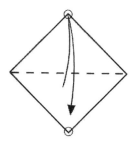

2 Fold and unfold in the half diagonally.

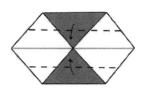

3 Fold and unfold in half.

4 Fold in the dotted lines.

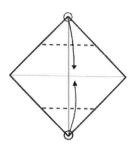

5 Fold to the center.

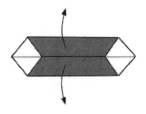

6 Unfold the layers.

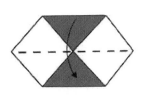

7 Fold in half.

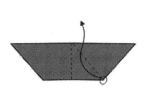

8 Pocket fold lifting the marked corner up.

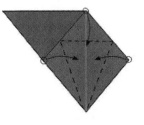

9 Fold the left, right and upper sides in the dotted lines and unfold.

39

 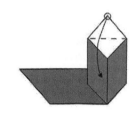 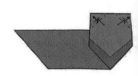

10 Fold the fron tlayer up using the creases.

11 Fold down in the dotted line.

12 Step fold to form the ears.

  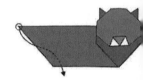

13 Fold up and then down to form the nose.

14 Fold and unfold in the dotted lines.

15 Do a pocket fold.

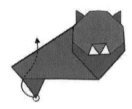 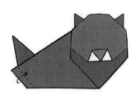 

16 Pocket fold up to form the tail.

17 Fold inside in the dotted line.

18 Finished Cat!

DOG

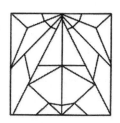

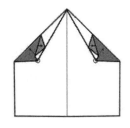

1 Start with the white side up.

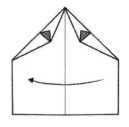

2 Fold and unfold in the half.

3 Fold the corners to the center.

4 Fold in the dotted lines.

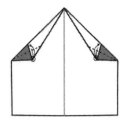

5 Fold and unfold in the dotted lines.

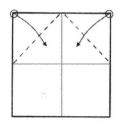

6 Fold inside to the marked point.

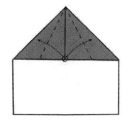

7 Slightly lift the triangle and fold in the dotted lines.

8 Fold in half.

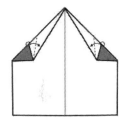

9 Fold up in the dotted lines.

41

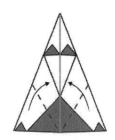

10 Fold inside.

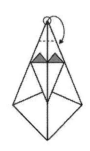

11 Fold back in the dotted lines.

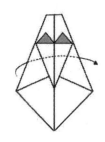

12 Fold in half.

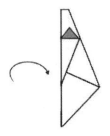

13 Rotate the model.

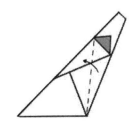

14 Fold the front layer in the dotted line.

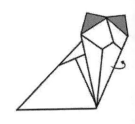

15 Fold the back layer backwards.

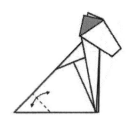

16 Fold and unfold in the dotted layer.

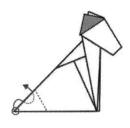

17 Pocket fold in the dotted line.

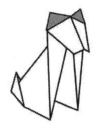

18 Finished Dog!

GRASSHOPPER

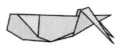 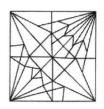

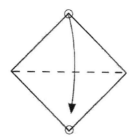

1 Start with the white side up.

2 Fold in the half diagonally.

3 Fold the model to the marked point.

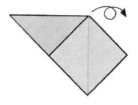

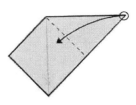

4 Squash fold the front layer.

5 Turn the model over.

6 Squash fold the other side.

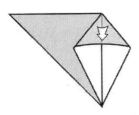

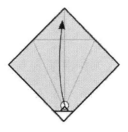

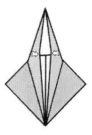

7 Fold and unfold the left, right and top corners to the center.

8 Lift the bottom corner up.

9 Squash fold the left and right sides.

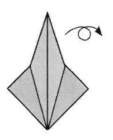 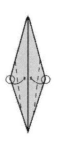

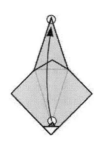

10 Turn the model over.

11 Lift the bottom corner up.

12 Fold the corners to the center.

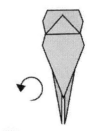

13 Fold in the dotted line.

14 Fold backward in the dotted line.

15 Turn the model around.

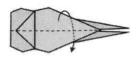

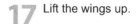

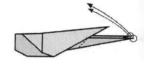

16 Fold in half.

17 Lift the wings up.

18 Fold the legs up in th dotted lines.

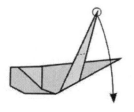

19 Fold down in the dotted lines.

20 Finished Grasshopper!

44

FLAPPING BIRD

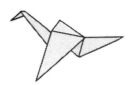 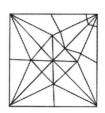

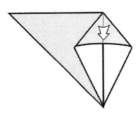

1 Start with the white side up.

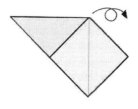

2 Fold in half.

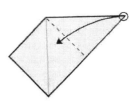

3 Fold the model to the marked point.

4 Squash fold the front layer.

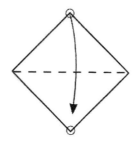

5 Turn the model over.

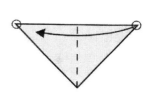

6 Squash fold the other side.

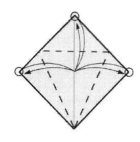

7 Fold and unfold the left, right and top corners to the center.

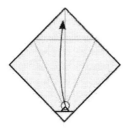

8 Lift the bottom corner up.

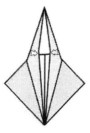

9 Squash fold the left and right sides.

45

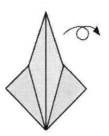

10 Turn the model over.

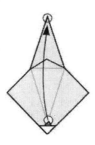

11 Lift the bottom corner up.

12 Pocket fold the front and back lacers in the dotted line.

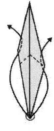

13 Pocket fold in the dotted lines.

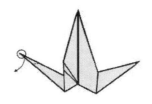

14 Pocket fold in the dotted lines.

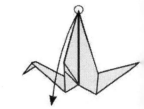

15 Fold the wings down.

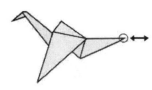

16 Finish Flapping Bird! Pull the tail to flap the wings.

ELASMOSAURUS

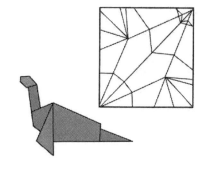

1 Start with the white side up.

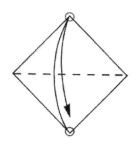

2 Fold and unfold in the half diagonally.

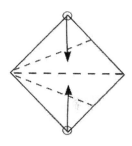

3 Fold the corners to the center.

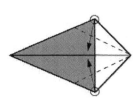

4 Fold in the dotted lines.

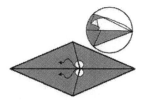

5 Open the pockets and fold as shown in the image.

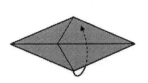

6 Fold in half.

7 Fold to the right in the dotted lines.

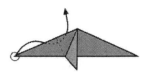

8 Pocket fold to the marked point to form the neck.

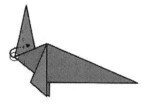

9 Fold inside in the dotted lines.

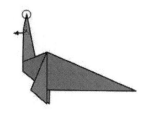 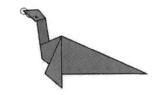 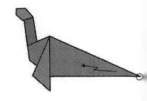

10 Fold the head down in the dotted lines doing a pocket fold.

11 Fold inside.

12 Do a step fold to for the tail.

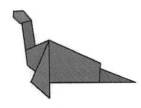

13 Finished Elasmosaurus!

SAMURAI HELMET

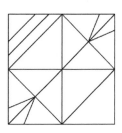

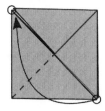

1 Start with the white side up.

2 Fold and unfold in half diagonally.

3 Fold diagonally in half to the other direction.

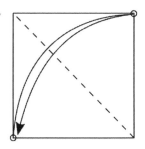

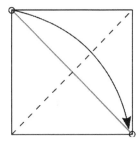

4 Fold and unfold corner to the top point.

5 Fold the corner to the bottom point.

6 Fold the opposite corner to the bottom point.

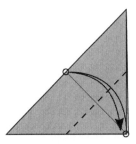

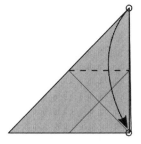

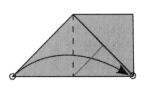

7 Fold the corner to the top point.

8 Fold the opposite corner to the top point.

9 Fold and unfold the flap to the right corner.

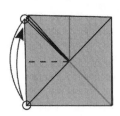 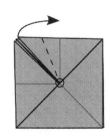 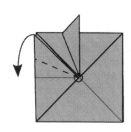

10 Fold and unfold the flap to the bottom corner.

11 Fold the flap to the right on the line.

12 Fold the flap down on the line.

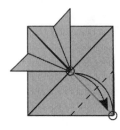 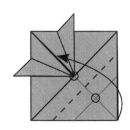 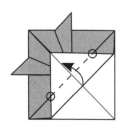

13 Fold and unfold the top layer to the top point.

14 Fold the top layer up according to the marked points.

15 Fold the top layer up again according to the marked points.

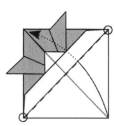 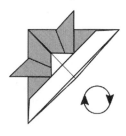 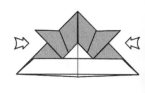

16 Fold the corner inside the model.

17 Rotate the model.

18 Push the sides to make the model 3D.

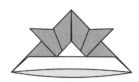

19 Finished Samurai Helmet!

CICADA

 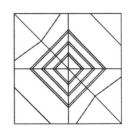

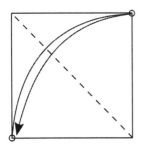

1 Start with white up. Fold and unfold diagonally.

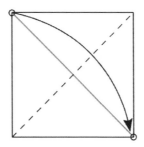

2 Fold diagonally in half to the other direction.

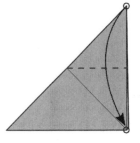

3 Fold the corner down to the bottom point.

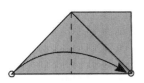

4 Fold the corner to the same point.

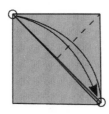

5 Fold and unfold the corner to the top point.

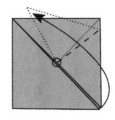

6 Fold the corner up according to the marked point.

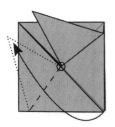

7 Fold the other corner up according to the marked point.

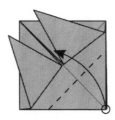

8 Fold the top layer up on the center line.

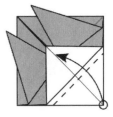

9 Fold the bottom layer up on the center line.

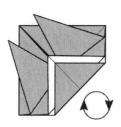

10 Rotate the model.

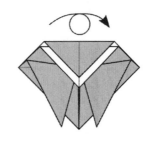

11 Turn the model over.

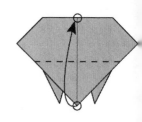

12 Fold the corner to th top middle point.

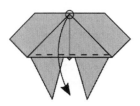

13 Fold the corner down leaving a little space between the folds.

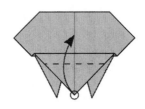

14 Fold the corner up on the middle line.

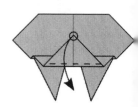

15 Fold the corner dow leaving a little space between the folds.

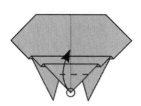

16 Fold the corner up on the middle line.

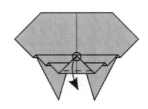

17 Fold the corner down leaving a little space between the folds.

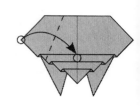

18 Fold the left edge or the center line.

19 Fold the right edge on the center line.

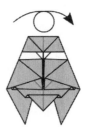

20 Turn the model over.

21 Finished Cicada!

DOVE

 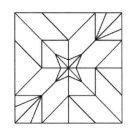

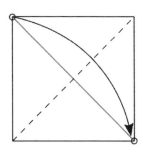 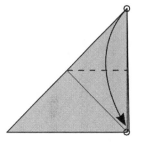 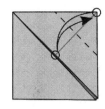

1 Start with white up. Fold and unfold diagonally.

2 Fold diagonally in half to the other direction.

3 Fold the corner down to the bottom point.

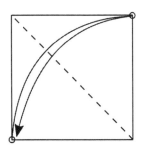 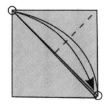

4 Fold the cornter to the same point.

5 Fold and unfold the corner to the top point.

6 Fold and unfold the top right corner to the marked point.

 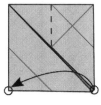 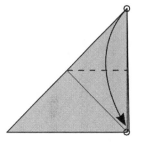

7 Fold and unfold the bottom left corner to the marked point.

8 Fold the bottom right corner to the bottom left corner.

9 Squash the paper down to make the model lie flat.

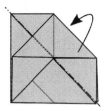 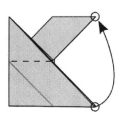 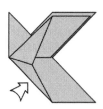

10 Fold the model in the right half by folding the right part behind.

11 Fold the bottom right corner to the top right corner.

12 Squash the paper down to make the model lie flat.

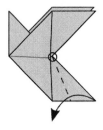 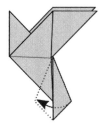 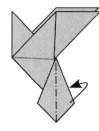

13 Fold the corner down according to the marked point.

14 Take out the hidden paper layer to the left.

15 Fold the right edge behind.

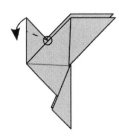 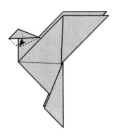 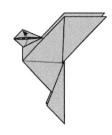

16 Fold the corner down according to the marked point.

17 Take out the hidden paper layer down.

18 Fold the bottom edge to the top.

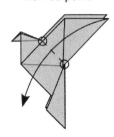 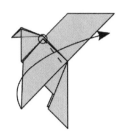 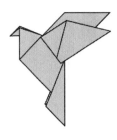

19 Fold the corner down according to the marked point.

20 Fold the corner back up according to the marked point.

21 Finished Dove!

CATFISH

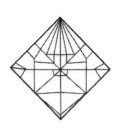

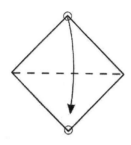

1 Start with white side up and fold half diagonally.

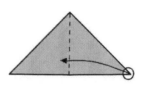

2 Fold in the dotted lines.

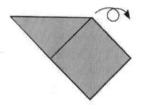

3 Lift the corner.

4 Fold in half.

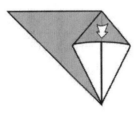

5 Do a squash fold.

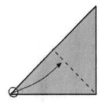

6 Turn the model over.

7 Squash fold the other side.

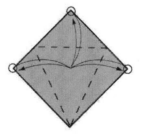

8 Fold and unfold the left, right and top corners to the center.

9 Fold in the dotted line.

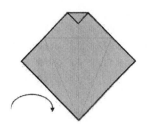

10 Turn the model over.

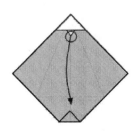

11 Fold the front layer down using the creases.

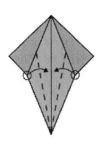

12 Fold the both sides the center.

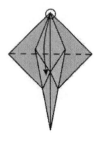

13 Fold in the dotted line.

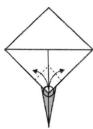

14 Fold diagonally up in the dotted lines.

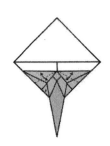

15 Fold and unfold in the dotted lines.

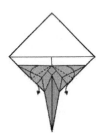

16 Fold down opening the pockets.

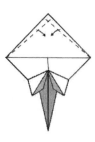

17 Fold inside to the marked point.

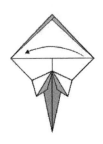

18 Fold in half.

19 Form the tail.

20 Unfold the model.

21 Finished Catfish!

DINOSAUR

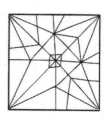

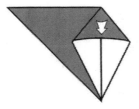

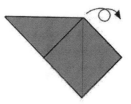

1 White side up, fold diagonally and lay corners on each other.

2 Do a squash fold.

3 Turn the model over.

4 Fold to the middle.

5 Fold and unfold the left, right and top corners to the center.

6 Lift the bottom corner up.

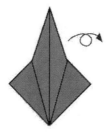

7 Squash fold the left and right side.

8 Turn the model over.

9 Lift the corner up using the creases.

57

  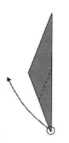

10 Fold down in the dotted line.

11 Fold in half.

12 Fold diagonally up form the legs.

 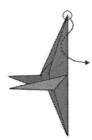 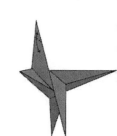

13 Fold and unfold in the dotted line.

14 Pocket fold to form the neck and rotate the model.

15 Fold and unfold in dotted line.

16 Pocket fold in the dotted line.

17 Fold inside.

18 Do a pocket fold.

19 Fold and unfold in the dotted lines.

20 Do a pocket fold.

21 Finished Dinosaur!

THE BASIC

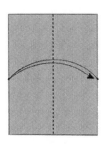

1 Fold and Unfold the paper in half

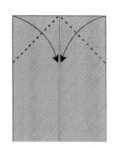

2 Fold the top two corners into the center line

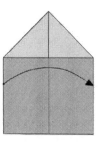

3 Fold the paper in half again.

4 Fold the top layer in half

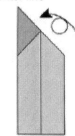

5 Turn the model over

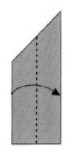

6 Fold the top layer in half

7 Open up the model by pushing wings up.

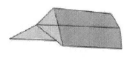

8 Finished basic airplane!

THE BUZZ

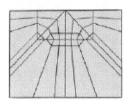

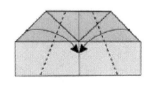

1 Fold and unfold the paper in half

2 Fold the top two corners into the center line.

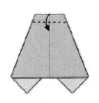

3 Fold the top down to the edge of the previous fold.

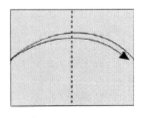

4 Fold the upper sides to the center line.

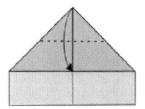

5 Turn the model over.

6 Fold the top about 1/2 inch toward you.

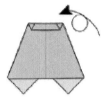

7 Turn the model over.

8 Fold the plane in half.

9 Fold the top layer to make a wing. The body has to be about 1/2 inch.

10 Turn model over.

11 Fold the top layer to make the second wing.

12 Open up the model by pushing wings up.

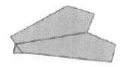

13 Finished buzz airplane!

The Sea Glider

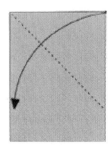

1 Fold the paper diagonally.

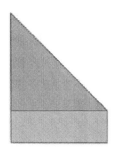

2 Cut off the extra piece at the bottom.

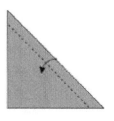

3 Fold the top edge over about 1 inch.

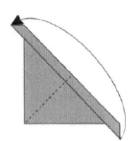

4 Fold the model in half.

5 Fold the top layer of the top edge over.

6 Turn the model over.

7 Fold the top edge over as the previous.

8 Fold out the top layer to create a wing.

9 Turn the model over.

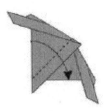  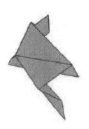

0 Repeat with the other side to create the second wing.

11 Add a few staples to the front to give the tip some weight.

12 Finished sea glider airplane!

Hunting Flight

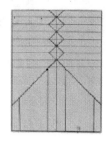

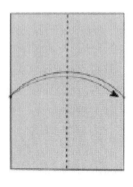

1 Fold and unfold the paper in half.

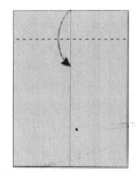

2 Fold the top edge down about 2 inches.

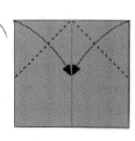

3 Fold the folded edge again.

4 Do the same one more time.

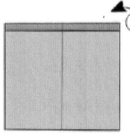

5 Turn the model over.

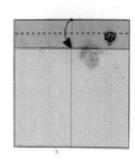

6 Fold the top two corners into the center line

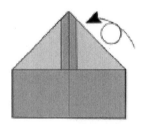

7 Turn the model over.

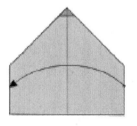

8 Fold the plane in half.

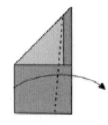

9 Fold the top layer to create a wing.

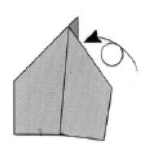

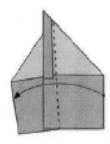

10 Turn the model over.

11 Fold the top layer to create the second wing.

12 Fold the top wing edge about 1/2 inch.

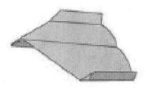

13 Turn the model over.

14 Fold the second wing in the same way

15 Finished Hunting Flight airplane.

Royal Wing

 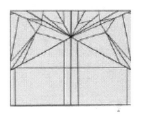

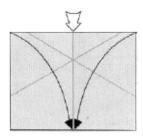 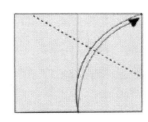 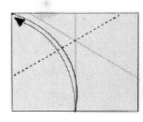

1 Fold and unfold the paper in half.

2 Fold and unfold the top right corner to the end of the central line.

3 Do the same with the left corner.

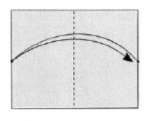 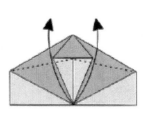 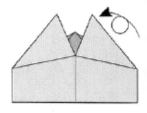

4 Fold both top corners to the end of the central line and push down the paper.

5 Fold the two flaps in the bottom up.

6 Turn the model over.

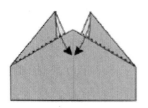 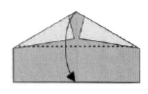 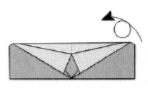

7 Fold the flap tips towards you.

8 Fold the model in half towards you.

9 Turn the model over.

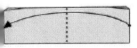  

10 Fold the model in half vertically.

11 Fold the top layer to make a wing. The body should be about 1/2 inch.

12 Fold the wing tips up.

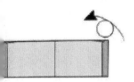  

13 Turn the model over.

14 Fold the top layer to make the second wing.

15 Finished Royal Wing!

Star Wing

 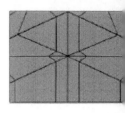

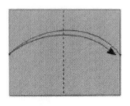 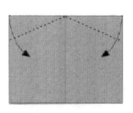 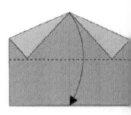

1 Fold and unfold the paper in half.

2 Fold the top corners to the central horizontal line.

3 Fold the model in half towards you.

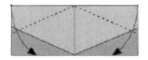  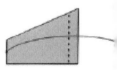

4 Fold the top corners to the bottom edge.

5 Fold the plane in half.

6 Fold the top lay to make a wing The body shoul about 3/4 inch.

 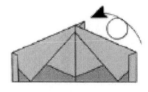 

7 Fold the wing tips up about 1/2 of an inch.

8 Turn the model over.

9 Fold the top lay to make the second wing. Spread the wing and tips.

10 Finished Star Wing airplane!

The UFO

 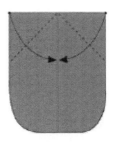 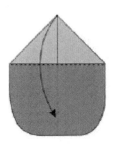

1 Cut out the bottom corners to round it off. fold and unfold it in half.

2 Fold the top corners to the center line.

3 Fold the peak down 2 inches before the bottom edge.

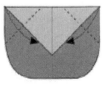  

4 Fold the top corners about half way down each.

5 Fold the top edge down about 1 inch.

6 Fold the model inhalf.

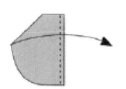 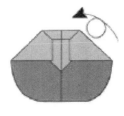 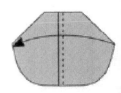

7 Fold the top layer to make wing.

8 Turn the model over.

9 Fold the top layer to create the second wing. Open up wings

10 Finished UFO
airplane!

V-Wing

 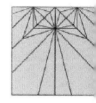

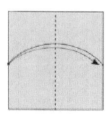

1 Cut off the bottom to make a perfect aqure. Fold and unfold it in half.

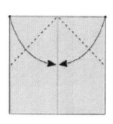

2 Fold the top two corners into the center line.

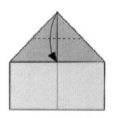

3 Fold the top down to the edge of the previous fold.

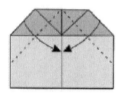

4 Fold the upper corners to the center again.

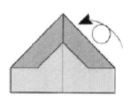

5 Turn the model over.

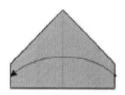

6 Fold the model in half.

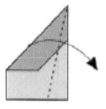

7 Fold the top layer to make a wing as shown.

8 Turn the model over.

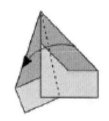

9 Fold the top layer to make the second wing.

10 Finished V-Wing airplane!

Gliding Plane

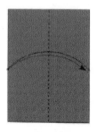

1 Fold and unfold the paper in half.

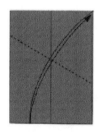

2 Fold the top right corner down to the center of the left half.

3 Unfold it and do the same with the left corner.

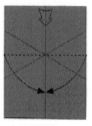

4 Fold everything according the lines and fold the center in.

5 Fold the outer flaps to the center line.

6 Fold the central part up.

7 Fold the flap tips from you.

8 Fold the again.

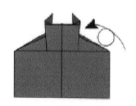

9 Turn model over.

10 Fold it in half.

11 Fold the top layer to create the wing.

12 Fold it one more time as shown.

13 Turn the model over.

14 Make the second wing.

15 Fold it one more time as the first one.

16 Finished Gliding airplane!

The Square

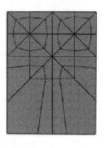

1 Fold and unfold the paper in half

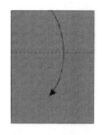

2 Fold the top down to create the half of a square.

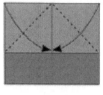

3 Fold the top corners to the center line.

4 Unfold everything back.

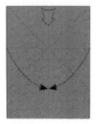

5 Fold the sides in and push the model down.

6 Fold the flaps up to the center line.

7 Fold the peak down as shown.

8 Fold the plane in half.

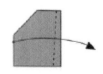

9 Fold the top layer to make a wing.

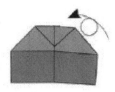  

10 Turn the model cover.

11 Fold the top layer to make the second wing.

12 Finished Square airplane!

White Dove

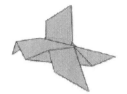

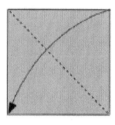

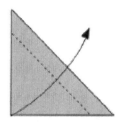

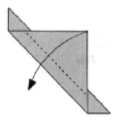

1 Fold the paper in half diagonally.

2 Fold the peak up leaving about 1.5 inches.

3 Now fold the top layer back as shown.

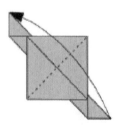

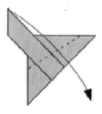

4 Fold the model in half.

5 Fold the top layer to make a wing.

6 Turn the model over.

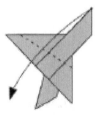

7 Fold the top layer to make the second wing.

8 Fold the bottom corner inside to make a beak.

9 Fold the wing as shown,

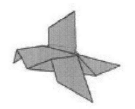

10 Turn the model over.

11 Fold the second wing the same way.

12 Finished White Dove airplane!

Eagle Eye

1 Fold the paper in half diagonally.

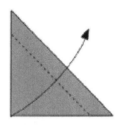

2 Fold the peak up leaving about 1.5 inches.

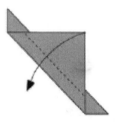

3 Now fold the top layer back as shown.

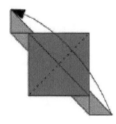

4 Fold the model in half.

5 Fold the top layer to make a wing.

6 Turn the model over.

7 Fold the top layer to make the second wing.

8 Fold the top coener inside to make a tail.

9 Fold the wing as shown.

10 Turn the model cover.

11 Fold the second wing the same way.

12 Put the plane with the wings up.And fold the bottom corner.

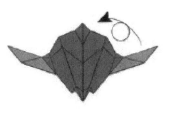

13 Fold the corner a little bit towards you to make a beak.

14 Turn the model over.

15 Finished Eagle Eye airplane.

Underside Plane

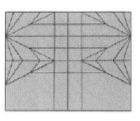

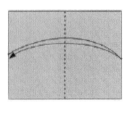

1 Fold and unfold the paper in half.

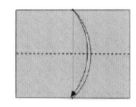

2 Fold and unfold the paper in half horizontally.

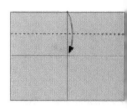

3 Fold the top edge to meet central line.

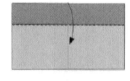

4 Fold the top edge at the central line.

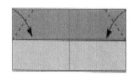

5 Fold the top corners to meet the horizontal line again.

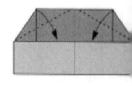

6 Fold the top corners to meet the horizontal line again.

7 Now fold the top edge to the same line.

8 Turn the model over.

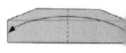

9 Fold the plane in half.

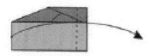 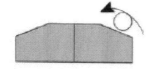 

10 Now fold the top layer to make a wing. The body has to be about 1 inch.

11 Turn model over.

12 Fold the layer to make a second wing.

13 Finished underside airplane!

Loop Plane

 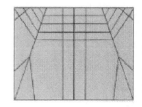

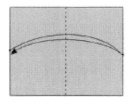

1 Fold and unfold the paper in half.

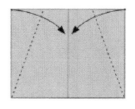

2 Fold the top corners to the center line as shown.

3 Fold the top edge down about 1/2 inch.

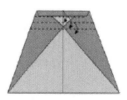

4 Repeat the previous step 3 more times.

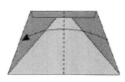

5 Fold the model in half.

6 Fold the top layer to make a wing.

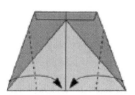

7 Fold the wings to make the flaps.

8 Turn the model over.

9 Fold the top layer to make the second wing.

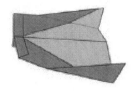

10 Finished Loop airplane.

Stealth Glider

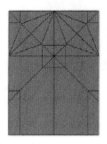

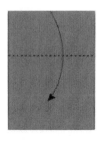

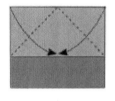

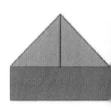

1 Fold the top down to create the half of a square.

2 Fold the top corners to the center line.

3 Unfold everything back.

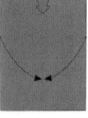

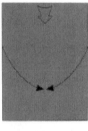

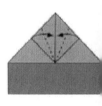

4 Fold the sides in to the center and push the model down.

5 Fold the flaps up to the center line.

6 Repeat the previous step one more time.

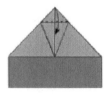

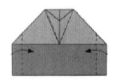

7 Fold the peak down.

8 Fold the slide edges.

9 Fold the plane in half from you.

10 Finished Stealth Glider airplane.

Spinner Plane

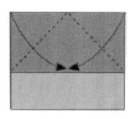

1 Fold the top down to create the half of a square.

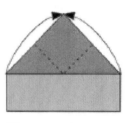

2 Fold the top corners to the center line.

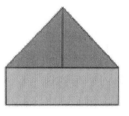

3 Unblock everything back.

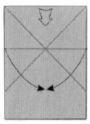

4 Fold the slides in to the center and push the model down.

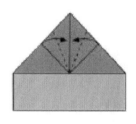

5 Fold the flaps up to the center line.

6 Repeat the previous step one more time.

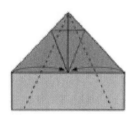

7 Fold the edges from the bottom layer to the center line.

8 Fold the top corner down.

9 Turn the model over.

10 Fold the plane in half.

11 Fold the bottom corners up.

12 Fold the top layer to make a wing.

13 Turn the model over.

14 Fold the top layer to make a second wing.

15 Finished Spinner airplane.

The Raven

1 Fold and unfold the paper in half.

2 Fold and unfold the paper in half horizontally.

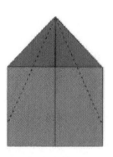

3 Fold the top two edges to the central line.

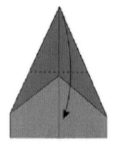

4 Fold the peak down.

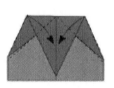

5 Fold the top corners to the central line.

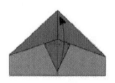

6 Fold the triangle flap up.

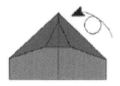

7 Turn the model over.

8 Fold the plane in half.

9 Fold the top layer to make a wing.

10 Turn the model over.

11 Fold the top layer to make the second wing.

12 Finished Raven airplane.

Light Spinner

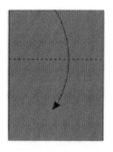

1 Fold and unfold the paper in half.

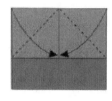

2 Fold the top down to create the half of a square.

3 Fold the top corners to the center line.

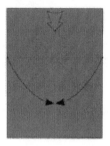

4 Unfold everything back.

5 Fold the slides in to the center and push the model down.

6 Fold the peak down to the middle edge.

7 Fold the flaps to the center.

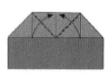

8 Fold them again to the center line.

9 Turn the model over.

10 Fold the plane in half.

11 Fold the left edges to make the wing flaps.

12 Fold the top layer to make a wing.

13 Turn the model over.

14 Fold the top layer to make the second wing.

15 Finished Light Spinner airplane.

Water Plane

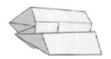

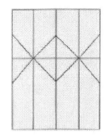

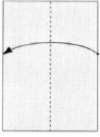

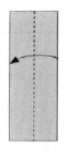

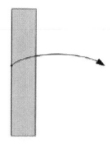

1 Fold the paper in half.

2 Fold it in half one more time.

3 Unfold the paper back.

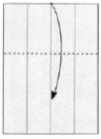

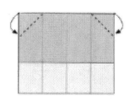

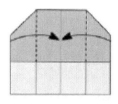

4 Fold the paper down about 3 inches before the edge.

5 Fold the top corners in.

6 Fold the top flaps to the center line.

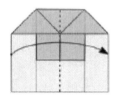

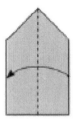

7 Fold the plane in half.

8 Fold the top corner in.

9 Fold the top layer as shown to make the wing.

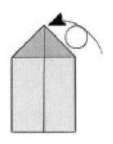

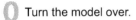

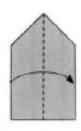

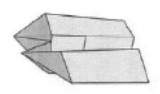

0 Turn the model over.

11 Fold out the second wing.

12 Finished Water airplane.

Cross Wing

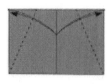

1 Fold and unfold the paper in half.

2 Fold in it half the other direction.

3 Fold the top corners to the center line as shown and unfold them.

4 Accordion fold the corners in.

5 Fold the top corners to the center line.

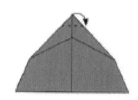

6 Fold the peak back about 1 inch.

7 Fold the model in half.

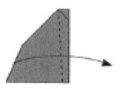

8 Fold the top layer make a wing.

9 Fold the wing tips.

0 Turn the model over.

11 Fold the top layer to make a second wing.

12 Finished Cross Wing airplane.

Made in the USA
Coppell, TX
22 October 2023

23176523R00055

Going for a Ride

A Journey to the Heart's Calling

Ginny Marshall-Frye

Copyright 2018 Virginia Marshall-Frye

ISBN: 978-0692113578

Printed in USA

Contents

Introduction: Where Are You Going?

Sometimes we have a certain perspective of how life is supposed to be or where life is supposed to take us. It's like going for a ride. Sometimes we have to speed up to get where we're going. At other times, we get stuck and frustrated—like being in bumper to bumper traffic. We look ahead of the cars and say, That's where I want to go, but why can't I see what's blocking the way? Why in the heck is it taking so long? Sometimes, we may take an alternative route or a detour that takes us off course, so we have to do a U-turn and get back in line and wait some more.

At times, its smooth sailing, and we immediately reach our destination. It seems like more often we hit a pothole in the road that delays our journey with a flat tire, or we swerve off course when a pothole suddenly comes up because we weren't really watching. We were driving half asleep.

We are the driver, and we either put ourselves in the driver seat and stay wide awake and in control, or we turn on cruise control and don't really focus on driving. Life just happens! Instead of creating our reality by the choices we make. Are you just blindly going about your life, or are you letting Divine guidance direct your course?

God is Spirit—and wants to be real with you. God wants to show you the way, the truth, and the life. God has a purpose in your life! God wants to help you drive your life by listening to your inner guidance to follow a life of truth.

This book is about one's journey and listening to the heart and following that call. It will hopefully help others to focus on what is deep in their hearts and listen to their heart and seek guidance from something bigger than themselves. We are all made with special gifts that we can bring into the world to help heal and make our world be a peaceful, loving place by being the light.

Chapter One - Trust the Journey

This is the story of how God has worked miracles in my life. God works miracles in all of our lives. When we awaken to the reality of who God is, we see miracles. You see, some believe it started with a big bang, but it was really God who created this universe. The big bang is something postulated by scientists that supposedly occurred 13.8 million years ago. All the matter of this world was compacted into a very small ball, and over time it expanded forming our universe. However, it takes more faith to believe in this concept. Look at how our animal kingdom and ecosystem work together in such an organized way. Is it possible that it all occurred just by chance? Or look at how the systems in our human bodies work together so interrelatedly—Is that just by chance?

When it comes to miracles, God gets all the glory for everything! Remember, he is good, regardless of what journey or path you are on! He did say Jesus was the way. God wants to show us the way if we only listen to that inner knowing or directing. It's not about religion or systems, but it's about knowing the way of the spirit and its leading in your life. Spirit is life!

God has been working in my life and calling me for a long time; even being born was a miracle. I had been in my mom's womb for only six and a half months when she gave birth to me. In those days, the 1960s, most babies at that stage of life didn't survive. I weighed two pounds, ten ounces; and dropped even more, to one pound, fourteen ounces. My mom told me that she told God that if I didn't live, she would never talk to him again. Laughing about it later when talking to her I said, "I bet you scared God by saying that!" Being born premature made me a fighter and I have been fighting ever since. They kept me in an incubator, but I made it. That was my first miracle! Staying alive!

God has his hand in our life from the very first second. So you see, it all starts with a miracle and you are the miracle!

While growing up—in grade school, then in high school, then in college—there was always a pull in me for spiritual things. However, I had to decide who was going to direct my path. There is a big difference between giving in to God and letting go, versus partially giving things to God.

In trying to go my own way, I was lost and needed to find God. I felt I was doing the best I knew how to, given my knowledge of God and what I knew. Honestly, I don't think I was following "the way" or the path he had for me. It was something my family did, but it wasn't my walk or path. For me to see a purpose to why I was born, I needed to be awakened to the truth. I needed to see that there was something more than my little life. God had a purpose for me and he has a purpose for you, too, if you are open to it. You just have to open your life to God and to what may be waiting for you out there. Sometimes, you can go willing and sometimes God can force things to happen. God will have his way!

My first encounter with God was in the sixth grade. Our family went to a high school auditorium to hear a man talk. This speaker wasn't just any man, but someone who had lived on the streets and was a reformed heroin addict. His name was Nicky Cruz. An evangelist named David Wilkerson had come to speak to Cruz earlier in his life when he was in a street gang. He said that Wilkerson had a fire about him, but also a **tenacity for helping those whom others had forgotten**. Wilkerson felt he should reach out to Nicky Cruz, and he kept after this street gang fighter to help him. He walked the streets with Cruz and showed him the love. Eventually, he helped him get on a different path.

Nicky Cruz talked to the audience about his hard start in life. He was abused by his parents and wasn't whole spiritually and emotionally. He felt the only way he could belong anywhere was to become part of the Puerto Rican gang life in New York City. While he was there, he gained leadership and power to make him feel like someone. He became hardened. There was one point at which Cruz even struck the evangelist, Wilkerson, and said he was going to kill him. However, Wilkerson kept showing him love, even when he was mean and disrespectful. Wilkerson was persistent, and the gang leader didn't understand why this strange man was concerned about him. You see, God had given Wilkerson supernatural love for these people, and showed love in many shapes and forms. You may ask yourself, how could he love this unlovable person? Wilkerson had a relationship with something bigger than himself, meaning Christ, and that gave him the strength to consciously love others.

Love finally broke through and Nicky Cruz came to know the love that Christ had for him. When he came to Jesus, he felt an overwhelming love and acceptance and cleansing of his soul. His life was transformed, and after that, he enjoyed telling others about the wonderful things God had done for him through coming to Christ. He shined and glowed with spirit. Cruz started a drug treatment center for others to get clean and be set free. God had made a difference in his own life that inspired him to help others change and find their way.

Cruz's story made such an impression on me that I thought, *Wow, if someone had that kind of love, someone who was hard to love, and he was affected, then there has to be something to this God.* After Cruz told his story, he asked people to come down to the front part of the stage and give their life to Christ. I went down during that invitation. I prayed the "sinners prayer." I made a commitment to Christ that was sincere and was real in my heart.

Nicky Cruz was a changed man. When someone recognizes that they have done wrongs, that is the first step, but the other is changing their ways. If someone can stand up after being a street person and make a 180-turn in their life, there has to be some truth to what Cruz was talking about. Intellectually, I believed, but letting Christ in seemed real. It resonated with my heart and it showed me the love of God. It seemed as though something opened up in me, and the journey started. I will always remember that day, January 12th. That was the second miracle in my life!

In my spirit, I knew that something big had come in, but I didn't know what to do next. How do you have a relationship with something unseen? Something inside of me thought by being a good person and loving God was enough, but looking back I realized that it really meant a changed life. It's really about giving your life to God and being a disciple, to live "not by my will, but thine."

Then in high school, things were a bit rocky at home, and I think I was trying to find my way. The wrong crowd was a part of my life; drinking and smoking and being rebellious, but that didn't last for too long. Deep down inside, I knew it wasn't the right path for me and I actually felt a bit guilty doing those things. There was some rebellion and resentment burning inside of me because of my life circumstances, but in reality, it was more than that—I needed some healing. I knew I was making a mess of thing and it wasn't what God really wanted for me. God wants us to live differently as his children.

The change started in my social network. One night when my best friend in high school came over, she overheard my mom talking about God with some of her friends and praying with them. I piped in with my mom and was excited that my friend was curious to know more about God. That day, my friend made a commitment to Jesus Christ and things started to change for us. We got involved with the high school Methodist Youth Fellowship and made friends with others who were believers and had wholesome fun together. I thought, *this seemed like a better way—to be involved with kids who wanted to grow in their relationship with God, yet have fun and be together.* Leadership was inside of me, and I made friends quickly. It felt like God had intervened in my life and what God wanted started becoming part of the plan. My friend believed as I did, and we started growing together in spiritual things and having fun together. She was like a second sister to me.

In the tenth grade, we moved from Northern Virginia to a little town outside of Milwaukee, Wisconsin. My parents moved our family there because they were spiritually led to the area. I was heartbroken about my parents' decision. Though I was happy to be moving closer to my many cousins and extended family in Wisconsin, I was sad to leave my friends. However, it was the answer to a prayer, even though at that point in my life I couldn't see it. My parents were involved in a Spirit-filled group—by that, I mean a group of people who seek God and humble themselves to hear what God's spirit is trying to tell them. Sometimes it's a deep knowing or intuition that God shows them or leading that shows them. If they hear God's voice, it is usually confirmed by a few people; the confirmation could be a vision or a word that someone hears and feels.

So, my father had followed the leading of God, and that's why we had moved to a town outside of Milwaukee. He worked with other people in the area that had a heart for leading people to Christ. A group of them organized something called "Jesus Rallies." These rallies would bring in big names to speak about the importance of coming to Christ. My mom soon opened a bookstore in this town. My brother, sister, and I were enrolled in elementary, middle and high school. I wasn't really happy about going to this new school but knew there was a plan in it, so we came across the states to see family and friends and make new ones.

One day, a cute boy in my homeroom class at school came over to the house. He introduced himself and invited me to a breakfast fellowship at the Fellowship of Christian Athletes. The wrestling coach, who had started the club, worked with the kids in the school.

A family in the community opened a local barn and they would have breakfast together before school. I was excited when the boy invited me to go, but when I found out they were meeting at 5 am, I had second thoughts!

It was a cold autumn morning with frost on the ground and a chill in the air. The wrestling coach's car pulled up to my driveway with all these guys sitting in the car. I think it was the whole wrestling team! They were packed in there like sardines, and it was a really big car—a Ford Fairlane. The coach introduced himself. Climbing into the car, I sat on the inside seat, a bit afraid that the door might burst open. The defroster wasn't working in the car, so every once in a while we would have to pull over and wipe off the windows to clear the view. The window had to stay open so the windshield wouldn't fog up and boy was it cold. It was literally freezing, and being the only girl in the car, I felt kind of scared.

We made it to the barn and had a great breakfast with fresh eggs, pancakes, homemade preserves—yummy food. It was a great way to be around kids who seemed motivated to learn about spiritual things. Kids who had goals and wanted to do something with their lives and encourage each other. As time went on, we became friends and we would talk about life. Before too long, we started having the weekly events at my house. We'd sing songs and talk about spiritual things, mainly how Christ was a part of our lives. We did things outside of the group as well. We went hiking, to food fairs, and did some toboggan runs on the fresh snow. It was great fun.

Time moved forward. I went to college and still kept a pretty clean life. I participated in sports, did school work, spent time with friends, and had fun and enjoyed myself. On the spiritual side of my life, I wasn't actively doing anything. You see, I believed in God, but I hadn't let God have full control of my life. I'd work on spending time with him, and then other things—such as life, would get in the way, and I wouldn't be focused on God.

Looking back on it, I probably felt I had achieved what I was supposed to in living the good life, but that wasn't the case. I felt as though something was missing. There seemed to be something deeper and I wasn't really sure what that was. I did have a deep interest in where others were spiritually, but only pursued it to a certain degree.

In college, I became involved in Campus Crusade and met some really good people, and was seeking God, but I felt there was something more. I also was involved in a church that was Bible-based, but I knew God was spirit and was raised to believe in the things of the spirit as a kid. I was seeking for more of God. Fortunately, while still in school, I found an interesting full-time job with sports medicine in it, and I ran the clinic at the pool. We had developed programs for people with back injuries, but we also talked with some of the clients about the deeper issues of life and would direct them to God.

There was a man with long brown hair named Robert who spoke to me. I still can visualize him working out on the equipment. While doing some exercises on the back extension machine, he said, "The Lord tells me he has a plan for your life and wants something for you, and wants to do something great." I sat there feeling suspicious and almost dumbfounded, not sure what to say. He invited me to go to a prayer meeting, and with some reluctance, I said I would.

At the prayer meeting, everyone was joyful and full of God and people were excited about what God was doing in their life. There was a group of people who would pray for others as they moved in the power of the spirit. One guy would say, "Here comes a wave, there it is . . ." and then all of a sudden, God spoke to me. It was as if heard God say, "Let things go" and "Be still and know that I am God." I thought, *WOW! I've never heard God like that before!*

After saying goodnight to everyone, I left the meeting and went to my car to drive home. While driving, I turned on the radio and the voice said, "You too can buy the tapes: BE Still and Know that I am God." Later on, after returning home, I opened my Bible to the scripture that said, "BE still and know that I am God." I laughed and said, "God, you have a sense of humor. I'll try to trust the process."

God was trying to let me know he was in control. During that time, there was a gal at the clinic who saw something in me, so I started sharing and talking about the Lord with her and started sharing my faith in Jesus Christ. One day a man I had never seen before came into the clinic. He started saying things about having a dream about her and described things that only God would know. It kind of freaked us both out, because it was real!

Later on, when I came from the back exercise room, he said to me, "Young lady, you have a calling in your life. You'd better come to my church and we will seek God's face to see what it's about. You have some decisions to make!"

Periodically, I did go to his church, but even before that, I knew God was working and pulling me in the direction of spirit. You see, God can pull us in a direction, but it's up to us to follow the lead. Then, there were a few things that took me off course, just like the detours when driving, and I stopped going to the prayer meetings. Looking back on it, I see there was a power trying to stop the divine plan in my life. I drove through some potholes and detours and got lost, and then I had to accelerate to get back on the main road and not waste any more time!

The church I was attending was a good church but I felt there was something more that was missing in my walk, my companionship with God. I started feeling the pull to possibly go somewhere else, and there was a leading. I went to a few local churches. While going to church, I felt God had been working in my life, but there was something I couldn't break through. I was depressed. Not a full-blown onset of depression, but I couldn't shake it. I didn't know why it was like this and I could function, but I couldn't shake it, and couldn't figure out what was wrong with me. I thought to myself, *I really don't have a lot of reason to feel depressed.* In reality, there were certain things I was achieving that seemed good. A lot of things were going well for me in my life, but the dark feeling just kept hanging on.

In my heart, I knew that I hadn't done things completely God's way, and I felt that it was clouding things over. I thought, *If only I do this or that, I'll be ok.* I tried those things and my life still wasn't working. The feeling wasn't going away.

One day a friend of mine that I confided in about my struggle asked me to come to her church. I said, "Come to your church? OH, I know about church!" I was being a bit sarcastic. But honestly, I knew that God could do miracles and I had seen amazing things happen. I knew God could do just about anything. Miracles were just a part of it. I grew up in a family where I had heard and seen miracles as a kid! I said to her, "I've seen miracles. My parents held Bible studies and prayer meetings and they knew all about that kind of thing." For goodness sake, my own parents had big evangelistic meetings and I attended them. My friend must have thought I didn't know anything and that she had the corner on the spirituality market. I kept refusing, but she was insistent. To be honest, she was driving me nuts and she wouldn't stop bothering me about going to her church. It got to the point where I wanted to say, would you just bug off? Finally, I gave in. I knew I needed some kind of support, and was willing to try.

So I started going to my friend's church, but with a skeptical way about me. I wanted to make sure that this was authentic. Sometimes, there is so much ranting and raving in churches that it's hard to know for sure if it's authentic. I sat there and watched to see what it was all about. I'd listen to the Pastor and see God work through her.

Towards the tail end of each service, there was a call for people to go up for prayer if they wanted to be ministered to. As soon as the service ended, I would beeline out the door, as I didn't want anyone to pray for me that I didn't know or feel comfortable with. I don't know, maybe I was scared because I didn't know what to expect, or afraid that my sins would be exposed and I would be found out. Nobody likes their dirty laundry to be seen out in the open!

At the fourth service, the Pastor of the church said, **"I think we are going to do something little different."** She continued, "We're going to have prayer in the middle of the service."

I thought to myself, *Oh my God, I can't run away anymore. I have to go up!* I felt very hesitant at this time. I knew in my heart and spirit that God could do those kind of things, but for me? To be honest, I was a bit unsure it was even possible. So, I took the step forward. Was I afraid? Yes. But did I need help? Yes, I did. I humbled myself that day, and God lifted me up.

While in line, I told God in my heart, "If you heal me, I will do whatever you ask me to do." I got up front and the team started praying for me and anointed me with oil. They hit on everything I was dealing with. Even things way, way back in my family history. I felt God's presence and then I went down, just like you see on the evangelistic TV shows where people are getting slain in the spirit. I thought, *Oh my God, this is happening to me. It can't be happening, this is too weird!* But it was! A feeling of freedom and a sense of peace and love came over me, and the whole painful thing I had been feeling was completely gone.

The Pastor asked me, "Do you speak in tongues?" I told her that I had in the past, but it had been a long time; I hadn't spoken in tongues since I was twelve. So, with that being said, she prayed for me and I immediately got them! It's like speaking a foreign language. You don't know what you are saying, but it builds up your inner spirit. I immediately got tongues. I had never experienced God's presence like that. I had experienced close encounters with God before, speaking to me in my head in prayer meetings, or I had felt a sense of peace, but nothing like this had ever happened.

It was *real*...I mean, real for me. The feeling of oppression came off of me and I felt released. It was a miracle! Another miracle! Everything I knew about what God could do truly touched my heart and something came into my spirit that I couldn't let go of. I remember going home that night and just crying and crying, and being so thankful because I truly felt the joy of freedom and release. It was as if the reality of God was now a real thing for me! I had never before experienced anything that real.

For about thirty days, I was on fire and wanted to tell others about the goodness of God and how he can reach them. I told my friends, coworkers, and even patients about it. It was so real to me. I wanted others to know the reality of Jesus Christ, that this energy of love, hope, and goodness could be yours and that God's spirit is life!

Now looking back, if I had been true to myself, maybe I wouldn't have had to go through this experience. God had always been in my heart and life, but never like that. I realized that submitting was the thing I had needed to do. In submitting, great grace came upon me and God started showing me the way!

Coincidentally, my appointment to get evaluated was that week. Of course, there really are no coincidences. When the receptionist answered the phone, I said I wanted to cancel my appointment.

"Do you need to reschedule?" she asked.

"No."

"How come?" she quickly responded.

I thought, *Do I tell her the whole truth? If I am honest, she is going to think, 'Whatever lady.'* But I decided to tell her the whole truth. Then I wondered, *how do I tell her?*

So I said, "Well, I am healed."

And she said, "Is it just like that?"

"I went to a church service and I got prayer and boom! I got healed."

Then she said, "What do you mean you got healed? I've heard of people giving their problems over to God."

I said, "It was more than that. I mean, more than giving my problems over to God. I GOT HEALED—completely and positively healed! A miracle!"

Then she said, "Well, give us a call if you change your mind."

I was ready to put the physicians out of business. Why wouldn't you want to tell others the good news? The GOOD NEWS that God is able to do these kinds of things and what the Bible spoke about healing people is true. When the disciples stood at the Gate of Beautiful, they gave Good News. You see, this person wasn't able to heal on his own accord. He needed those that had the power to glorify something greater than themselves. God gives us the power to do greater things, but he first heals us. God is powerful, God is good, and God is able!

I was on fire! On fire because I knew that what had happened to me had totally changed my life. For about a month, I was on a cloud and telling practically anyone about it, sometimes, telling people that really didn't seem to care. But I thought everyone should know the truth, because this God stuff is real and I wanted others to know the reality of what I had experienced. God's love guided me out of the wilderness.

By going to that church, I knew in my heart that God had started something moving in me. Over time, something changed in me. The things that I had participated in the past seemed futile and I wanted to be part of a community and do what God wanted. I began to have all kinds of creative ideas about ways to reach out and help others learn about this God I knew. I felt others needed to know about the Good News.

Chapter 2 - Something New

The great commission of Jesus charged us to be a part of healing our world and making it whole. It charged us to restore what God initially intended, especially the Garden of Eden, which was the way of peace, love, and wholeness. God started working in my life and I started spending time with others in the church, as well as seeking ways to help others.

Wanting to speak hope and life to a group that so needed life, or even hope, was something that was deep in my heart. I wanted to give the hope and life that needed to be shown the way, not bang people on the head with ideology or dogma, but sure words. Words that gave life.

Shortly after my experience at church, I walked into the home of some friends watching football. They looked up and asked, what was new with me! *What's new with me?* I thought. *I'll tell you what is new with me!* I wondered if I should tell them the truth, or just give them superficial information. After pondering it for a while I decided to tell them the truth.

"I'll tell you what is new with me," I said. "I got healed. I got touched—and I've been made new."

One of the guys said, "Wow, that sounds pretty interesting. I believe God can do things like that."

They kind of laughed at me, but even while laughing, they listened to my truth. These friends had a long history of watching sports with me and doing things from time to time. One of the guys, Dave, seemed interested in what I was talking about, so thought possibly I could get my friend Tom (who I went to church with) and liked tennis to join and play with Dave and me. I thought it could be a way to bring that into the mix, without bringing him to church. After we were done playing tennis, Dave told us he had just been diagnosed with cancer. I told him how sorry I was, but didn't know what else to say. I really didn't think to do anything about it, or even pray about it.

As my friend Tom and I started walking away, he said to me, "Maybe, we should go pray for Dave."

I thought for a moment and agreed. We turned around and headed toward Dave. When we caught up with him, Tom said,

"Dave, would you mind if we prayed for you for your cancer?"

"That would be great!" he said.

So, there we were on a sunny day outside of Dave's home. His brother in law (with a Jack Daniels Whiskey t-shirt), his sister in law (with a similar Winston cigarette t-shirt), Dave's wife, Tom, and I—all of us had our hands on him and were praying for him. All hands around him asking God to heal this man. All different backgrounds, but believing in one power, joined together for another's good. After the prayer, we congregated outside of his home and talked. Dave had gone back inside with his wife.

Dave's wife screamed from the kitchen window, "Dave felt something go through him!" She looked at me and then said, "Actually, it felt like an electric energy went through him like he has never felt before." A power source.

Dave said, "I am healed, I think." "Wow," he said, as he shook his head, "that is powerful!" He kept saying that over and over." His eyes were as big as saucers! Then he said, "I've never felt anything like that before. Never in my life."

I thought, *Wow, maybe it was God's power working through us to do a bigger thing! Maybe God wants to reveal his glory, today, to do greater things through his people if people are open!*

I kind of laughed inside, thinking of the crew with the liquor and cigarette brand shirts laying hands on this guy. It was just like Jesus going to the highways and byways to talk to people and being no respecter of persons, and his works were made manifest. Another miracle! God was redeeming his miracles through his people! You see how God works in our everyday life.

I thought, *Boy, God knows these people's hearts.* It just so happened that everyone who was there that day had an experience with God, but they went their own way. You see, God knew the fruit it was going to bring, but I had no idea that almost everyone there hadn't been going to church in a long time, but had a deep background to God and felt that.

This experience changed Dave. The next Sunday, Dave's whole family was at church. The sons, his wife, and the brother and sister-in-law. They weren't conventional churchgoers, but God knew their hearts. Later on, Dave started playing the drums and before too long, he was speaking to others while driving taxi cabs. He had a call to do something greater in God's kingdom, too, as he had the heart to share!

So you see how God can cause a ricochet effect so that others can be affected. When God is in it, you do bring him glory. More was brought to him. To this day, Dave will never forget that encounter no matter where his life goes. Whatever happens, once that seed is planted, it is there for good!

God started giving me other kinds of opportunities. Most of the time I would just sense in my spirit, so I would reach out. Some of these sensations would be like fire on my face, and a tingling warmth in my hands—a knowing or feeling the spirit. In some churches, they call it "the anointing." I didn't understand what the anointing was at first, but I was learning. It's God's presence. Sometimes, it would just show up while out doing my business or living life. Sometimes, I'd be out and about when it happened, and I would think, "Not now God, I have to other things to do!" But I would obey and do what I felt I was supposed to do. Many times I would go in half-heartedly, but it would always turn out to be a blessing! You know when you are supposed to do something, because it resonates with your spirit; it will feel like a blessing as the spirit is life. It's something more than ordinary. It was being led by the spirit.

The spirit, when it comes, can feel like electricity going through someone's body. It's actually power and God's spirit is supposed to feel like that. The word for it is *dunamis,* a feminine noun, which means the power to achieve miracles with might and strength, and the ability to perform.

CHAPTER 3 –

BEING A TRAILBLAZER

After going through the experience with Dave's awakening or being touched by God, I kept attending church, and something in my heart of hearts spoke to me about helping others. What I heard was that other people should be helped, not only those who were downtrodden, but also people like me who needed to be found. If you only listen to your heart, you can do something big if you feel inclined. You can be a trailblazer. You just have to know your assignment!

You may wonder, who or what is a trailblazer? Webster's dictionary defines it as: "a person who blazes a trail for others to follow through unsettled country or wilderness; a pathfinder. A pioneer in any field of endeavor." Trailblazing applies to something new that helps people in society, whether it's a scientific invention or something of a spiritual nature—a new way.

Christ was a trailblazer—one to show the way. He didn't give his life for us to go back to our old ways. He changed people and put them on a different path . . . a path that leads to life!

One time, I was invited to a baseball game and I was planning on going, but a few nights after the invitation, I opened up a devotional to read. I felt as if God was saying to me, "I didn't show you my glory for you to go to a baseball game." I think what God meant wasn't that I shouldn't go to the game, but that there is something grander if we let go.

Sometimes, we have a way and God has a better way. Jacob in the Bible had to let go of control and see the plan God had for him to give God ultimate authority and control. You see, God had a plan much greater than Jacob ever thought. Jacob wanted to control things instead of relinquishing control. That calling is the best way because it will take you to places you never dreamed of, and attaining may be what is in your heart in the first place and that will give you the peace of God.

What does it actually mean to have a calling? Does it mean giving up your life for something greater, something with purpose, something that is of value? There is something around the corner of newness that God wants to show you and make a way for it. Sometimes we have to be the trailblazer, to create a path to show others the way. Sometimes we have to birth things because people don't know where to start. Sometimes it's about creating the path that says, This is the way! Or God puts something on your heart to open yourself up and create something new!

The trailblazer Robert Kennedy once said: "Few will have the greatness to bend history itself, but each of us can work to change a small portion of events. It is from numberless diverse acts of courage and belief that human history is shaped. Each time a man stands up for an ideal, or acts to improve the lot of others, or strikes out against injustice, he sends forth a tiny ripple of hope, and crossing each other from a million different centers of energy; and daring those ripples to build a current which can sweep down the mightiest walls of oppression and resistance."

Let's be the hope and the love! Let's blaze trails for others!

Harriet Tubman was in the clutches of slavery, and when she found freedom, she helped rescue thousands of others who were slaves. Harriet Tubman freed slaves, and she also freed many white people when they realized they were enslaved to the institution of slavery. Harriet Tubman took a negative and brought about a positive!

That's how it is at times with people: metaphorically speaking, they are slaves to their addictions, their lifestyles, the things that they idolize, and before you know it, they are in bondage and they need freedom. Sometimes people don't even know they are trapped and set in a certain motion. They need to hear the truth so their eyes can be opened to know this is the way!

How can someone know a different way unless someone shows them? How can anyone change unless someone who has been enslaved to a belief learned how to help themselves?

Billy Jean King was another trailblazer. She opened a door for female athletes. She was the first woman tennis player who pushed women's sports to a new level when she did the Battle of the Sexes and played against Bobby Riggs. She pushed the limits and opened the way for women to participate in all kinds of sports. She started a new wave!

Trailblazers believe in themselves. It's hard to believe that publishing *Harry Potter* was ever considered to be a risk, but J. K. Rowling's struggle to find someone who believed in the book as much as she did was a tough one. Even as a single mother living on welfare, though, Rowling wouldn't let any number of rejection letters stand in her way. She refused to stop believing in the work she had created. One year after landing an agent, she finally got the call from a London publisher. The rest is history.

Jesus Christ, the great trailblazer, spoke of a different way. He was the one that showed the way. The Divine One. The Anointed One. He spoke to the multitudes. God's Son gave Life and compassion. He only did what the Father told him to do. He died for mankind to redeem him from the curse of death and Sin. He gave people hope and help when they were stuck and needed direction. Christ changed people and put them on a different path, a spiritual path that leads to life. Christ delivered people from demonic oppression, healed people emotionally and physically. He touched those that others wouldn't touch. Shepherd of the sheepfold. The Way, The Truth, and the Life. The Greatest phenomenon. He gives strength to the weak. He makes the foolish wise. He is immortally graceful, and His goodness is limitless. Jesus came humbly as a servant, but could have called on 10,000 angels. He is my example and he is my King! His love is infinite; he is graceful, he is good, he is limitless... He strengthens those who are weak and shows them the way!

We first have to believe that we are human beings and that we are under a greater power and Authority that rules the earth. It's in knowing Christ that we become immortal. In the image and new beings, beings and beckons of light. Yes, the universe is for us, yes, the divine and God is for us—but are we for him?

Do we realize that we are yet sinners that need to come to the fullness of who God initially created us to be? That by acknowledging that God is in control and at his word the heavens shake and the earth collapses! We come under the authority of God and we then become something new. We have to realize that Christ came so we could have a redeemed relationship and take on a new mindset, new way, new world, and makes all things new! Sometimes we have a way, but there is a better way!

We have to spur on ourselves and others to make a new path or a new way. What happens if you are supposed to be a path maker, or something is put in your heart to do something bigger? In the quietness of our hearts there could be many possibilities to do something great. Something bigger than just living life and doing whatever someone else does. Do you think there may be a better way or something different for you? Do you always have to follow the masses?

Sometimes we have to unplug to find out what that "something" is. I watched a documentary about men in Syria called the White Helmets. These were ordinary men who had professions who chose to do something different for a bigger cause—to help victims of bombs or trapped behind rubble and such who had to be dug out to safety. These men all came from different professions: a baker, a pharmacist, a tailor and then they became a White Helmet to save people in disastrous situations and tremendous pain. One of them said, "My goal is to save as many people as possible!" He had a mission and he was focused to accomplish his task to save people's lives!

In order to save others, these men had to have to have a servant's heart. I personally think that the greatest example of a servant's heart was Jesus Christ. He gave his life so we could have life! Just like the white helmets that gave their lives for something greater than themselves.

These Syrian men had a vision. They knew what inspired them and gave them fulfillment. Though there was a plan, a bigger purpose. None of them probably thought they would be doing this, but something in their destiny said yes, and they chose to do it.

Sometimes we have to go step by step. It may not happen immediately. It's not what we may want or think it may be. Sometimes we have to Dream Big and look at all the possibilities. If you don't have a dream you will most likely never get there. What do you really want? There is a scripture that says a man without a vision dies. Do you have a vision and what do you want to achieve? My vision was to say GO!

"And the Lord said unto the servant, Go out into the highways and hedges, and compel *them* to come in, that my house may be filled." Luke 14:23

CHAPTER 4 - GOING TO
THE HIGHWAYS AND BYWAYS

The way of the spirit means coming outside of our agenda, getting off the ride we have taken up to that point, and looking for the DIVINE agenda. What is the next ride we're supposed to have on our journey? How is it supposed to happen?

Sometimes you may not know what your Divine agenda is, you can only open your heart to prepare and be led by the way. The way for me was walking with the unlovable. I felt in my heart that I was supposed to help those who are less fortunate than myself.

During the autumn of 2003, while in a little town in the Pacific Northwest, I was reading a devotional by Smith Wigglesworth. In that devotional, it talked about helping the incurables. The next morning when I picked up the newspaper, the front page headlines said: GO TO THE HOUSE OF THE INCURABLES. I was stunned. Could you call it a coincidence or was this a divine synchronicity? Most likely, as it was a confirmation of my guidance. What does that mean? I wondered. There are houses with incurable people, places for people who have incurable diseases. There are those who are sick or have incurable mental diseases—homeless and abandoned people. Which population were you talking about God? I asked.

Later that week, while driving downtown in the community where I lived, I saw a place that I had only heard about. This was a place for people with AIDS—a house of the incurables! It was a place where AIDS patients lived. Many so-called religious organizations didn't even know how to deal with this particular population with love and kindness.

From reading about AIDS, I knew that it was an untouched area that many so-called believers didn't know how to deal with. I realized that it was rampant in Africa. I felt I needed to go to that house. The house for the incurables. So I went to the house and asked one of the staff, "Do you have volunteer programs?" They said yes, and had me fill out some paperwork and did a background check.

To be honest, I didn't know what I had in common with the people living in the house. I really knew very little about the AIDS population, I only knew it was an untouched group that many didn't even know how to work with. I went there thinking, what do I say to these people? They are going to think I am trying to convert them to my way of thinking. However, I realized I was supposed to step out and do it because God had shown me to do that!

Love can be an unspoken solution to many needs without even bringing in religion. Sometimes, it's just our actions that point the way and sometimes it's speaking a kind word. That is what they needed—love. Love to the unlovable. I needed to be with them. I knew God would show me when I should say something. So I spent time with these men. I watched movies with them. I played games with them. Nothing came up. I kept asking God to show me. There was one guy at the house who I swear looked like the serial killer Charles Manson. It was very scary! He was a really strange person, with little trolls in his room, and I thought, *Please help me, Lord!* I actually found this man to be harmless in my interactions with him. I comforted him in this time of being vulnerable about some hard circumstances in his life. But there were times when I would say to myself, what the heck am I doing here? Did I really get the right impression or guidance by coming to this place? This is weird.

One night we were talking and playing games and sitting around the table. One man told me his story. The story that shared with me was that he was molested as a young man, and I thought, *There it is!*

I felt God's presence. It's a tingling feeling, and you just know that it's God. I knew this was the opportunity to speak the love of God. I told him, "You know God never meant that evil thing to happen to you. The God I serve is a God of love, and mercy, and grace, and it wasn't his plan at all for that to happen." He just looked at me with amazement with the kindness I was stating the truth. Evil happens in this world of ours, and people do detestable things. Those things destroy a person's being and don't give them true life. Sometimes people blame God for the evil that happens in the world, but it is never, never God's plan, as God is good. Always Good!

When evil destroys the core of who a person is, God wants to rebuild them with Good things. So God was showing me and giving me an opportunity to show this man his love. That is all I said to him during my visits. After a certain time, I felt my assignment at the house had ended. I had shown love to those unlovable people, those that others won't touch. We can feel when it's time to move on. Sometimes you have to look at the fruit to see if it's worthwhile and there may be another way to go!

I didn't Bible-thump them or try to convince them of anything. Personally, because I had a faith-based life, I think they had a false idea of how I might act or present myself. I felt that I just needed to be myself and God would show me the way to deal with them.

Sometimes you have to sacrifice, but with the sacrifice comes great gain, a feeling of fulfillment, a sense of accomplishment. In his image. I brought LOVE, and hopefully somewhere deep in their hearts, the words spoken were life, and that is all I can do. Speak Life!

God's next step was to take me on a path on the streets. I heard about a local ministry in town that worked with these kinds of people, and I decided to go down to the streets. In going down there I met a few people. I thought it was kind of interesting—another synchronicity, as it started out with me making my first commitment to a man who was a gang fighter on the streets. God knew way back, when I saw Nicky Cruz speak about his life, how it had touched my heart. And God put that in my heart to birth something. It was a full circle thing!

There was a hot dog stand for hot food, a table for clothes, and then people preaching outside to those that came down to the event that met every Saturday evening, rain or shine. There was a group of people who would go to the homeless camps where these people lived. The people helping would first meet up and stuff their backpacks with socks, underwear, and food and then walk the streets. Looking around at the homeless individuals, there were all different types of people—from those who had all their belongings in a grocery cart to those who looked like they hadn't taken a shower for weeks at a time. It gave me a deeper love for humanity and for each human soul. I watched everything going on around me to figure out what they were doing. I felt a little out of place, and uncertain of what I really was supposed to do. I thought maybe I just needed to take it all in, and so I stood around and met a few people and observed things. I knew in my heart that I went there because I had felt led.

I met two people who said that they worked in the local soup kitchens to help these poor people. It turned out that the soup kitchen was right around the corner from where I worked. I thought it sounded like a great opportunity to meet some of these folks and get to know them as people.

So, I started driving over to the soup kitchen on my lunch hour to see these people and established relationships with others who needed help. The kitchen had local food donated to feed these people and many of the volunteers worked hard to help those less fortunate. Many of the regulars would go over there to do their laundry, get some food, and then take a shower. This place seemed more than a soup kitchen for many of them as it was a place to congregate and connect with their peers.

In going there I'd sit down with the people who came in. Some came sporadically, and others every week. They had lunch two times a week with showers, and a place for those who needed to do laundry could. I found out about their lives, and how they lived. Some of them lived in the woods, some had lived on farms, some lived the lifestyle of homelessness. Some of them, due to poor life choices such as drugs or alcohol and others, chose the life they were living because they didn't want responsibility.

Some had no family and may have been there because they had isolated themselves, or alienated themselves from family because of the lives they led. A lot of these people didn't want to live the way others had decided to live, but wanted a more carefree life, and to keep things simple.

Many of them knew about God and criticized the church and how religious dogma has infiltrated our thoughts and beliefs. I was a bit surprised at how much these homeless folks really knew about God, and the extent that traditional religion had encroached on the simple message of the gospel.

During this time and season, it really taught me to love the unlovable, and that God could redeem their lives if they would be ready and willing to turn over their lives. It was about showing them God's love and then seeing if they would receive it. In turning over their lives, it would be coming to God and searching out his way— the path that leads to love, the path that leads to forgiveness, the path that leads to life and peace. Even if they were alone, God would be with them. I won't pretend that I have this whole love thing mastered. I have tried. Sometimes we protect ourselves and don't give Love out, because we feel we must only give to those or be kind to those who deserve it. This is ego, and ego has attachments and conditions.

Love is everywhere and we must free ourselves of our demands to really love. Is this easy? No, it's not, but we can consciously try to move in that direction and become more loving. God is love and that is the character of God. For he so loved that he gave us his son! Some of us don't really know that kind of love—a sacrificial love that is poured out to us. When we receive that love we only want to give back.

In going to the streets and helping the people there, I wasn't sure what to do. At first, I wondered, what am I doing here? But God told me to go there and I listened, even though I really wasn't sure how to go about it. I learned by doing. It was a culture shock, and I was a bit lost myself while trying to find and help the lost. I remember walking the streets thinking to myself, where do I start? who do I speak to, and about what?

This was foreign territory, but when I went there, I felt God go with me. The closer I got to the place where they had the regular Saturday activities for the homeless, the more I felt God's presence. What a wonderful confirmation. I knew I was supposed to GO, but I was really running with the wind, because I had no idea what I was going to do when I got there.

I started by asking people about the different things they were doing to help and looked for where I felt led to help. There was a clothing area with free clothes to give away. I met a few workers who spent hours sorting the clothes and laundering them and getting them ready. There was also a food truck in which they served hot dogs, pizza, something warm. They also had music, as well as preachers speaking something to encourage people. There was a group of people that stayed by the facility, and a group that would go to the camps, and others would walk along the streets to help people.

We would basically get together and see how many groups there would be, and then decide where we would go. At first, I went a couple different routes to compare the difference. Initially, we would get their backpacks ready full of socks, underwear, food, and clothing. These camps were interesting, to say the least. Groups that would go to the camps, usually had a leader and the group consisted of men and women. There were a lot of students from the local college that came, too. I had no idea where these camps were, so we walked the trails to find the places where these volunteers would go.

I can still see the group of us, with our headlights on our heads, tramping through the woods. Some people had tents to live in, some slept in a corner of a building. Some were open to talking, some were just trying to stay warm, and some lived in their cars. These were the people that needed hope because they had no hope or love. Some of them really surprised me. I really didn't know what to say, but I could tell them about God and what he could do for them because of what he'd done for me.

A few weeks went by and I started thinking about a friend who probably had a heart for the same kind of things that I did. It's nice to do work like this with someone else who you feel is supposed to go with you. Sometimes people don't even realize that quite possibly they were called to the same thing. Sometimes people have to say let's try it, and see where it goes. Honestly, before I was called, I didn't know things like this existed in the town where I lived. I felt like my friend Mel would enjoy helping the street people, but I also knew that it might compete with watching his sports events.

Mel was a man in his sixties. He had gray hair and rosy cheeks, he was almost six feet tall and a little husky. He had an outward appearance of a tough demeanor, but inwardly, he had a heart of gold. He had his own struggles growing up. He never felt approval from his family because of his wayward ways. He had a drinking problem in his past, but had found God and felt the love that he needed. He had taken a different path and identified with some of these people, so thought that he may be open to it.

I called him one night and said, "What are you doing?"

"I'm catching the Huskies game," he said.

I said, "How about you come with me to the streets tonight and check it out?"

He said," I don't know, it's pretty cold out there. Aside from that, the Huskies are on, and I was planning on watching them.

I said," Just bundle up, and put on some boots—you will like it! "

"Ok," he said hesitantly. "I'll meet you downtown."

Mel came downtown wearing a big purple and yellow Huskies shirt with jeans and a parka to keep him warm. I showed him around, and he saw a few people that he recognized, as he had worked at the soup kitchen we both had gone to. We met with the people who were running it. Interestingly, it turned out Mel knew someone in leadership. The leadership person said, "Did you know

Mel, it was your testimony that brought me to Jesus Christ." It blew him away and knocked his socks off and gave him the best blessing!

Mel had a soft side to him also. He grew up in the Pacific Northwest. He had a coffee stand and became friends with the people who bought coffee from him. The locals and the fishermen were his friends. He had a passion for photography and capturing the beauty of creation. The walls of his home were filled with his photography. He had pictures of everything from weddings to beautiful sunsets, and a crane swooping down on the water, to the majesty of the mountains. He had created a place where he found peace and serenity. His little place.

Some people didn't get to see all the sides of Mel like I did. Sometimes he'd get grouchy, but he was evolving into someone who was a changed man. A man who was redeemed from the path he had taken, and his journey was to tell others the good news of Christ and his love. He was a quiet soul, but down deep, you could see the essence of who he was, and it gave him joy encouraging these people that he could himself have easily become.

After a while he started calling me saying, "Hey there Ginny, are you going to go to the camps tonight?" He started choosing to go out to see these people, instead of staying home and watching the game. He started wanting to go and would drive and say things like, "Hey, I have my van all packed up and READY TO GO!"

One night I called him and said, "Ok, tonight we are going to the camps."

"I'll drive!" he said.

I thought it was really cool that he wanted to go. Mel and I asked the leadership, "Where do you want us to go tonight?"

They said, "Go to the place of the guide."

"Ok, I'll take him there."

We started gathering a few backpacks and got on with it. We stuffed the backpacks with Bibles, socks, underwear, and food. We drove over there and we had two stops that night. It was a really wet and cold night. However, we would trounce out into the woods with a flashlight to find our way in and out. It was a great feeling helping others and speaking life to their situations.

At the first place we went to, there was a big field between us and where the people were camped. You could look across and see the line of trees and nobody would know that behind the trees were camps full of people with entrances to each area.

As we walked across the field, we found a worn path that people walked on. There were areas we had to walk around because the water was so high from the rains. We used our flashlights to see where we were going. I spoke with Mel, "Ok, here is the first place." I could always tell it by the abandoned grocery cart. I said, "Let's walk in." There was a path and sure enough, a campsite.

At the campsite, there was a laundry line, a table, dishes, and a tub full of water for washing dishes. There was a lawn chair, as well as garbage bags all over the place filled with things. There was a pitched tent, but we looked around and didn't find anyone. There was another tent full of food and beer cans and other things. I felt so bad that someone would choose to live that way. It seemed like a reflection of someone's inner life—messed up and needing cleaning and organizing, just what Christ can do for us.

I thought possibly they were visiting their neighbors in the next camp. I said to Mel, "Hey Mel, it doesn't look like anyone is here. Let's go down to the next site." We headed for the site just down the trail.

When we got to the new area, we saw three tents set up. There was a lazy boy chair and three people sitting by the fire. I never thought I'd see a lazy-boy chair in a homeless camp. One of the people was named Barry, another Ken, and the third, Brian. They were excited to see us because they knew us and recognized us from the Soup Kitchen. One of the guys happened to be someone I knew, too. They were all about the same age, from mid-thirties to possibly late forties. Their place was clean and tidy, which surprised me, and they invited us in.

We offered them clothes and food and they gladly accepted. We sat around the fire and talked about them, and who they were. We offered prayers. They gladly accepted! We all held hands and each of them spoke a prayer from their hearts. They spoke either with gratitude or just making a request. Over the few years we worked with them, we got to know each of their stories. It makes me very sad to think that these men could have survived that we worked with, but they didn't. I grew to love them all in their different unique ways.

One man had come from a family that loved him, but he had some alcoholic tendencies that affected his life. One didn't have a belief in God or a higher power for whatever reasons. He felt there were a lot of hypocrites in the church, and I felt he needed healing from his past experiences. The other man had chosen the lifestyle of living on the streets, even though he had people who were willing to help him. He was kind of footloose and fancy-free, but down deep they all needed to be loved. They all had some upbringing in the church.

They needed wholeness, as somewhere in their life they took a turn that left them empty and cut off from all that life could give to them. I started to care about them and pray for them to find themselves and to find their way.

I could tell that they saw the love we had for them. Even in their peculiar ways of not fitting into society, they needed more. They were nobodies that were just making it through life. They could have chosen to create something different for themselves, but for whatever reason, they hadn't. I was there to hopefully point the way, to show them that there was a better way that leads to life.

Many times we went into situations in which we weren't sure what might happen. Would people come out and talk to us or not? Sometimes we went into areas where there could be drugs or encountered situations that could be dangerous. We tried to use wisdom in going into such places with discernment.

One time I saw a little girl in the camps, and felt bad that she had to grow up in such an environment. I spoke to her mom, but she didn't believe there was another way. She said it was the best she could do. We tried to help the situation, but there really wasn't a lot we could do. We always spoke hope and light to them. We became their friends and showed them love.

Many of these homeless folks felt nobody really cared if they lived or died. We did our best to show them a different path. Some of them even came to church with us, but some of them choose the same path instead of the one that leads to life. I grew quite fond of many of these people.

Here is a story about Barry, one of the homeless men I worked with. Barry struggled with depression. He seemed like a nice guy when I first met him, clean-cut, not someone who you would think would live on the streets. He had recently moved to the Pacific Northwest and lived in one of the camps that I went to.

One day I was out walking and something said to me in my spirit to go visit him. He was having an extremely hard day and was down. He had a daughter that he really wanted to see, and I could see the love he had for her. I thought, *How can I help him?* What could make his day? I thought of getting him a bus ticket to go back home to see his daughter. So I went to the Greyhound bus station and asked if it actually went to his hometown and it did.

Something inside said, do it! However, I thought to myself, *If I do it and he doesn't want to accept it, what will the outcome be?* So, I thought, *I'd better ask him.* I went to his camp and explained to Barry, "I am not doing this out of pity for you or anything. I am doing this because God put it on my heart to help you. Maybe you will see that God really does care about you and loves you." He kept saying, "Gin, you don't have to do this!" I said, "I want to, please, let me help you." So, he graciously accepted my offer. I went down to the station to buy him a one-way ticket. As I went to drop off the ticket my eyes saw a bus pull up from the local area. Out came three guys with their arms loaded with beer. My first reaction was, what I am doing? Should I rethink what I feel I am to do? I asked, "God did you really want me to help this man?"

I felt it in my heart to do this, and to bless this man and not to judge. Hopefully, years down the road, he will look at this event and remember. We just plant the seeds and others come along. I hoped this would be a seed that would speak to him years down the road. I went into his camp and gave him the ticket. He said, "I don't have any luggage." I went home and got an old suitcase and he was so pleased to have it.

The day came and off he went. To this day he didn't become a convert, but I feel it spoke to his heart and his spirit. He is now off the streets, and Mel and I got him some things to help furnish his apartment. He was very appreciative of how we helped and remembers us.

Occasionally, he calls me to just check in or ask me how I am doing. So years down the road, he does remember how someone reached out, and how God was reaching out in a LOVING way, a way he could understand. Hopefully, he sees the light in all of it. We are supposed to be light to a world that is dark.

CHAPTER 5 - Reading the Signs

There is a time and a season for everything. After working with the homeless organization for a few years, I felt it was time to start something new. I was sensing something was happening in my spirit and I needed to move on. Sometimes we don't know where things will take us, but we have to trust the journey. For whatever the reason, we may sense that a change needs to be made and, often, it's so we can do our own thing. In order to create something new, I had to let go of what I had previously experienced working on the streets. That's often the hardest part—

letting go of the past experience or the thing we are so used to. However, we have to realize that God is love and there is always a plan in it. By letting go, I could allow the new thing to come and just let it come together. Sometimes we have to listen to our own intuition about something and what the main goal and objective is. My intuition was saying it's time to move on. Even though all the signs were pointing that way, I had to force myself to do it. That is how my next group mission started.

I started meeting with a group who were potentially interested in doing a street mission. It all flowed together amazingly well. It was a handful of people and we organized what we thought we would need to get the ball rolling. We decided we would need the basics: food, clothing, sleeping bags, and coffee, and we worked together to set things up. At our meetings, we not only brainstormed, but we also prayed for the individuals that we had already had been working with on the streets. Some of the people in our new mission had gone out on the street before and knew these people. Many times we just went with the flow of things. I asked people to do certain things: one person checked into making a sign, one checked into places we could hand out the food and clothes, one checked into different places that would be interested in helping donate food. We also asked the congregation at the churches we were attending if they would bring in clothes or sleeping bags to donate to the cause. One couple donated a huge number of sleeping bags.

One of the guys, Barry, in our group made a really cool banner that said: "Taking it to the streets." We put up the sign where we were meeting.

Someone else made postcards that said: "Taking It to the Streets – Coffee and Fellowship." Starbucks donated all their day-old bakery, and a local bakery gave us bagels and baked goods; even one of my neighbors brought in apples every Sunday morning. It was so exciting to see how this was pulling together. We saw the momentum building and the vision was there, so we kept it up, and soon things were happening! Many people from all different types of background showed up at our meetings.

Typically, we would have coffee and bakery to offer, with guitars and bongos playing from time to time. Most of the time, we would open up with a team of women dancing, and then have preaching, and praying afterward. Typically I'd preach something that I felt inclined to talk about, and occasionally, others would give a testimony or two or something that God was doing in their life. Some people would just mosey on through, come to listen or have coffee as they traveled through town. Others would come week after week. Some of these individuals really felt it was their church. One guy would ride his bike down to the spot every week.

Many seeds were spoken to the people who came. Some knew the truth already, but some didn't. Regardless of whether they were passers-by or people that came frequently, I hope and pray that in their hearts of hearts, they understood that these things were given to minister and give them hope—to speak to their hearts and give them something to focus on to possibly change their outlook on life. Sometimes, we would convict them and we had many conversations at those gatherings that were thought-provoking.

We helped countless people, including homeless families who had lost everything. We helped one family by providing linens and things for their new home. I remember two girls who were hitchhiking through town, and they had no money to return home. We gave them bus tickets, as well as clothes, as all they had were the clothes on their backs. We also gave them kind words and tried to speak life into their situation. Regardless, of what happened to these girls, I am sure they will remember that day when they were stranded, and someone gave them a ticket back home—and maybe they will pay it forward. Maybe it will be something they look back on and realize God's grace.

That is the way of God. When we are stranded, he gives us a ticket back home. Sometimes we get so caught up in what we're doing that we get lost on a path that doesn't lead to life; but there are good people who will show us the way. Hopefully, the spirits of the folks who came to us were awakened. Some of these people considered this meeting place their sanctuary. It was a place they knew they would be supported, a place they were given truth. I still remember one day standing out in the rain with someone from my church; I was holding an umbrella over us, so I could speak from my notes. We went there rain or shine—and it rains a lot in the Pacific Northwest. They were counting on us!

One day, a man came up to me and said, "Hey, Pastor." I thought to myself, *Pastor?* Though in truth, to him, I was his Pastor—a lady on the streets speaking to the people, and maybe I was the only Pastor he knew. He said, "There is something I need to let go of, can you help me with this?"

I said, "Sure I can."

"There is a friend of mine and I have a brick that he gave me. I have been holding onto this for years in remembrance of him," he said. "This brick represents a burden that I have been carrying around with me. I need to give it to someone else, so I can move on from what it represents. He has passed away and I felt so much grief with it."

When he gave me the brick, it was like a confessional or like something that was taken off his back. Clean, made new. Whatever occurred, I know he felt some sort of release from the burden of it, so he could move on. That is what God does; he cleans us and makes things new. We give him the burdens of the things we have done wrong with our lives, some call it "sin" or whatever, and then we can let go. Sometimes we need to let go, so we can learn the lessons and embrace something new. I took his brick and think I still have it somewhere, but with it, I didn't just take his brick, I took his grief. This man felt like a weight was lifted from him and he was healed emotionally.

He knew God and his love, but sometimes we have to serve as God's hands and feet to help people see and feel it. I was there at the right time to speak hope and life to him when he needed it. I hope and pray that this man is on his path of discovery and hope, as I am sure he was healed and whole from the meeting. I don't know how he even heard about us, but he did, and came down every Sunday morning. Sometimes we would wonder where he was, and then from afar, we would see him coming toward us on his bike. I can still see how happy he was to be there with us! It was his truth for the week, and he'd talk with the others about what he learned and he would tell his friends. We'd see him come down on his bike and you know I think we made a difference in his life. Who knows, maybe he looks back on those times, and those nuggets of truth or experiences, and it has formed him in some way. If we hadn't taken the steps to do something different to help these people, it may never have happened.

My friend Mel, who was a part of this ministry, said to me, "You know I feel the most fulfillment when we go on the streets and help those people. It puts a spark in my heart and makes me feel I am doing something incredibly special aside from my regular life, like I am doing something to impact others. I feel like I am giving back and this brings gratitude to my soul."

Another gal we poured love into was named Red. She had red hair and blue eyes, with one lazy eye. She was pregnant and living on the streets and had nowhere to turn. We helped her and her little one get a head start on life. One of the other girls who had a heart for those who were unfortunate had a baby shower for her. We treated her like she was one of our own, and at the shower she got needs met for her and her little one.

Years down the road, she moved into an apartment and was cleaning her life up. I bet that little girl is about ten years old by now. Who knows? Maybe her mom told her child about the baby shower we had for her mother to help her get started. We stood with her as she started her life and as time went on she went on her way and we lost contact. I always wondered what happened to Red and that little one. I hope and pray she remembers the love and life we gave her because we knew God. I hope and pray she is on a different path. I hope and pray for that baby who is now a youngster. I am sure Red will remember the love that was shown to her to help her on her way and point a new way. You see, in this work you can only point the way; others have to take it.

Mel felt grateful when he was giving back, and by doing this work. If we just focus on our problems and our own lives there isn't much hope in that. Sometimes we have to listen to our hearts and listen to what brings gratitude or fulfillment to our soul so we can give back.

Some of the people that we spoke to never made it. They knew in their hearts we were speaking the truth to them, but either their lack of willpower or direction, they couldn't follow the way. Their cycles had them trapped and they couldn't see their way out of their mess.

Taking It to the Streets of Costa Rica

I had a friend who had connections in Costa Rica and was taking a group down there to help people. I thought it would be interesting so I joined the group. Going on the streets in a foreign country turned out to be very different than working with street people in the U.S. I had been to Mexico and Tijuana and saw poverty there, but the ghettos of Costa Rica have greater poverty than I had ever seen. It was an eye-opening experience in many ways, not just working in the ghettos, but also because of the country's different lifestyle and culture.

The countryside was beautiful and I loved the simple culture of the place where I stayed while there. It was refreshing, waking up in the morning and looking out at the lush countryside. I stayed with a woman who had opened her home to guests. She had chickens in the backyard and fresh coffee beans harvested from the trees in her yard. It was a simple life, a quiet life. No television, not a lot of distractions. Something the people in the U.S. could learn from. It was quite comical because she couldn't speak English and I only spoke a few words in Spanish. One night I was trying to communicate with her through hand gestures, and finally, I had to call her daughter on the phone so she could translate for us. I took the bus to the local places we were going to either to work with the kids in the low income areas or help do the work in the church. It was a simpler life and I liked that.

Every night, my host made tortillas for me to eat. All her family lived on the same block, and sometimes family members would come over and eat with us. However, none of them spoke English so I just smiled and nodded my head. She did most of her interaction with her family. They all lived in one city, San Jose, and they were close to each other. One night she invited me to a family gathering where they had loud Mexican music and everyone was laughing and hugging each other. I just sat there and smiled, because I could only say, "Hola, and "Me llamo es Ginny."

While there, I went to speak with the children of the area, and participated in a local church. Oh my goodness the temperature was

hot. We would go to the playground and play games with the kids as well as love them. We would do skits with a few of us gals and talk about God with them. It was endearing to see the sweet little faces praying, so pure, and moving. Many of the kids came to our activities. They needed hope. As you can see from the pictures, the kids with heads lowered and eyes closed were saying unspoken prayers to a God that listens.

We also went into the ghettos and saw shack after shack with dirt floors, with a blanket covering the entrance. When we went into these modest homes, we were surprised to see a big screen TV in the living space. I saw strings of electrical wires running throughout the ghettos. The homes had tin roofs, and often there were gaps in the roof where the rain could easily come inside. People with kids gathered around our cars to get clothes for the little ones, as we were the only means of getting their needs met. It was as though we were bringing light to their broken world. In giving them hope this expanded our hearts, outside of our world.

Going to a place like this where people are in such need opens up one's eyes and helps us to appreciate all the blessings we have. Many times people don't experience anything outside of their comfort zone to expand their hearts. Most of us have so much in our country and many people don't even realize it. Gratitude and thanksgiving go a long way, and it is important to recognize these things. Going to Costa Rica and living among these people did something to my heart and expanded my ideas, but more importantly, it allowed me to be grateful for the many things I had.

In our culture, we have certain values and beliefs that tell you what's important and how you should live your life. What kind of car you should drive? How many kids you should have? What do you do with your time? There are all these messages out there and which ones do you listen to? Did you ever wonder if there is something outside of this norm? Some way to live other than what is expected by society? Maybe it's time to ask yourself some questions: Are you doing things because it's expected of you? Or do you really think about what you are doing based on what's important to you—because you feel you have a purpose or destiny?

Believing we can do something outside of what we've been told to do is sometimes important for our growth. Do you want to be like everyone else or do you want to be someone who is uniquely you? Do you want to be something beyond what you can imagine? Did you ever stop to consider that you may have the answers inside of you to do what you are really itching to do, or called to do? It's easy to follow what everyone else is doing. Not always so easy to follow your own calling.

You see, to help others on the journey, I first had to come out of what I thought my life was about. I had to let go of my agenda and listen to the higher calling or way. I had to listen to my heart. There is a scripture that says that by losing your life you actually save your life. There was something instinctively inside of me that "just knew." There has to be a drive inside of you a sense of purpose that makes you alive and gives you character and a light in this world.

Sometimes we have to unplug to find out what that "thing" is. It helps to look at examples of people who followed their heart and felt called to do extraordinary things. The documentary called "The Zoo Keeper's Wife" tells the story of a family who sheltered Jewish people in their zoo during the Holocaust. They saved over 300 lives. It's astonishing! There are many stories about people like these who rise above their circumstances and fears to help others in times of need.

Like the zookeepers, I felt something in my heart that reached out to the broken and hurting. It's not just because I was a good person, it was because when you feel the love from the divine creator you want to give back to our world. You want to heal our world and make it a peaceful place. My first calling was to go to the home for people who contracted AIDS. I had been praying about what to do next with my life and felt something nudge me, as I opened a book that directed me to go to the House of the Incurables. You see, I saw the signs and went after them. It was a synchronicity of events that led me to that place. The church had no idea how to work with these individuals, and I thought, *Okay God, if you are showing me to go in there, I will.* So, in I went. I didn't know what I had in common with these people. No idea, but I know it was an untouched group that many didn't even know how to work with.

My street mission eventually stopped for various reasons. Some things are just meant for a season; some things are supposed to happen in order to birth something new. My purpose was about showing others the way, the truth, and the life... It was about helping those who others have discarded and giving them hope. Christ says it's more blessed to give than receive.

After the streets shut down, there was an empty spot in my soul. I knew I was a doer, and sometimes we are supposed to just let go and move on. I knew there was something else I was supposed to do, but I wasn't quite sure what it was. I would ask God to give me a sign: "What do you want me to do?" During that time of searching, I'd pray for the people I knew and became more involved in the church I attended to get new insight on God's ways and path for believers.

Before long, I found a sign—though it wasn't what I would ever have imagined I was looking for. While driving around downtown, I suddenly felt a sensation as I passed the local jail. I felt a fire, a warm tingling on my face. It does say in the Bible that those who are led by the Spirit are sons of God. I had to trust that I was being led. I remember thinking to myself, "Not the jail, not the jail. I don't want to go to the jail!" Finally, after a few months, I gave in to the inclination and the nudging that said, yes, this was my next step. I thought, *How in the heck am I going to get into the jail?* But you see, I was divinely guided, so I was shown the way and things came together. Things don't have to make sense; if it's supposed to happen, it will. You just follow the signs!

One day while coming into work very early in the morning, I saw a couple that I knew. This man was someone I hadn't seen for years, and he so happened to be working for the Sheriff's Department. I was surprised to run into him, because he was the only person I knew of who could help me make a connection at the county jail. So you see, there are no coincidences when God wants something to happen. Look for the signs, as they will appear; the synchronicities will happen. Follow those leads and they will take you where you want to go.

We exchanged phone numbers. At the time, he didn't know who I should contact. He said he'd give it a shot and try to think of someone. In the meantime, I had lost his phone number. I searched high and low for his number. I looked in the phone book, but couldn't find anything under his name. Then I recalled Jamie telling me it was his cell phone number. I thought, *Shoot, how can I figure this one out?* I decided to call his mom, as I am a personal friend of the family. I spoke to Joann, explaining that I wanted to find Jamie and was looking to do volunteer work in the jail.

She said, "I can give you Jamie's phone number, but also, there is a lady who is part of my study group I attend, and I believe she is involved in the jail."

I said, "Please ask her about this, and tell her about me." She was glad to help and said she would let me know. Another synchronicity—an event telling me to keep following the signs.

When I called Jamie, he said he had no idea where I should start looking. He suggested a few churches, but I thought to myself, *See?* God knew me and worked with me and even used the situation of losing his phone number. If I hadn't lost his number, I would never have called his mom, and she was the one who opened the door for the connection I would make. I waited to hear back from Joann. She called me a few days later, and said, "I spoke to the woman in my study group, and she just happens to be in charge of all the women who work in the jail that give Bible studies." I thought, *You have to be kidding!* Here was another sign showing me that I was being led.

God sure works in mysterious ways, but if I hadn't looked for the signs, I would never have found the way. The woman called me and we got together. She asked me why I wanted to go to the jail. I was completely honest. I didn't go into a long explanation about why I felt I was supposed to go to the jail. I just told her that I was led by the spirit to go in there—I felt called! To be honest, I really didn't want to go in the jail, but was willing to be obedient because God showed me that it was important for me to do it.

The woman in charge asked me to fill out some paperwork and she said, "That is good enough for me." They did a background check on me, had me fill out a questionnaire, and the rest is history. I signed up. Just like that! No other questions asked. I wasn't required to take any classes and I wasn't given any preparation to work with the prisoners.

She told me initially that there were no openings, and I would have to wait and see how I would get in. However, God knew that in a few weeks down the road, her husband would pass away and there would be an opening. So, there you go! The opening presented itself, even though it was an unfortunate circumstance. She gave her resignation and left the area to live closer to her kids.

At the jail, I was assigned to work with a woman named Kathy. I ended up knowing who Kathy was, as I knew her mom. Kathy and I went to the jail together for almost five years. The first time I went inside the building was a scary experience. I certainly didn't know what to expect. I tried to look confident, but deep down I felt a lot of fear. I was always on guard. But as time went on, I became more comfortable in that environment and knew it was the right thing for me to be doing.

It was a wonderful experience. We were assigned to work with the women. Typically, Kathy and I would pray for the ladies before we went inside. We met them in a small, low-security work center for women and men in a mid-sized Pacific Northwest town. I believe there were six tanks. In those tanks there were bunks alongside each other, as well as a shower and a stall for the toilet. Usually, there was a TV in the room. The women wore red covers as a uniform, and the guards had a station.

There was a long hall and a library, and at the end of the hall, there was an area to the right with a kitchen and to the left was a recreation area, as well as a counseling room and the isolation rooms. Week after week, we went in every Monday to speak life and truth to the women. We would switch off weeks; one week Kathy would speak and one week I would speak. It was interesting, as some of the women would be very open and close to making a decision, but others would be reluctant. It was usually not the same women every week, and our success was often dependent on the environment we walked into. Sometimes the women truly had the motivation to learn about Christ and his ways, and other times they would just want to walk down the hall to get a glimpse on the fellows in the other tanks. I'd boldly say, "Keep your eyes forward, keep your eyes forward...DON'T LOOK in the tanks!"

Usually, I'd try to pick up on the spirits of the ladies when we walked in; that would give us more discernment to know who was ready for us to pour into. You see, Christ didn't pour into everyone, just those ordained for that season. We spoke to countless people, and I ran into all sorts of women at the jail. There was a wide variety. I saw pastors' kids, people who had their first booking into the jail and were pretty scared about being in there, someone who was a repeat offender, some prostitutes, and some who couldn't get a grip on their drug addiction or other self-destructive cycles. I tried my best to look at each situation with clean eyes and a pure heart and understanding without judging their circumstances. I always tried to redirect their steps to spiritual things. Many times, they would go off track while I was counseling them and talk about their stuff or drama in the tanks. I would always do my best to steer them back on course, and help them reflect and learn the lessons they needed to, so they wouldn't repeat them. Many of them just needed forgiveness from the shame they experienced, and I could offer that.

Many times, it was very sad to work with these people, because a lot of them didn't really have a good start in life and they had deep pain. They didn't have anyone who really cared for them, and many had experienced so much abuse that they didn't know how to live healthy lives.

While praying for these people, I often felt led to pray a certain way to get to the root of their real issue. Sometimes the root had to be taken out, and it was up to them whether they would return to the issue that was revealed to them. Sometimes I saw real change, and sometimes, it was only temporary. Many call it a jailhouse conversation!

Sometimes I felt really bad, knowing it may be the only time I could potentially rescue someone from themselves. I remember at one point working with a girl who was in her early twenties, who knew that if she went out on the streets, she would probably start using again. I tried desperately to get her into a house that was faith-based so she could have a fresh start.

Something in my spirit said: She needs to go into that house. We talked a lot and she was adamant about going to stay with her sister. Maybe it was common sense on her part, but I honestly thought it wouldn't be wise for her to return to her sister who used drugs, too. I thought to myself, *Please don't do it, your sister uses, and it won't be good for you.* But the woman thought she would be ok, that she could make it. One week later, she passed away from an overdose. My inclination was right, and I felt so sad that she made that choice in the journey of her life.

We all have choices, and sometimes it's hard to know the best choice to make. I asked her to pray about it and to seek God. I question how much she really did turn to God, because things may have worked out differently for her if she had. It was very sad as she was a pretty girl, had a young child, and had a lot of potential. We all have choices and God wants the path that leads to life.

On a happier note, we had a success story at the work center. One of the girls I can see clearly in my mind: her name is Jessica. She was bright, had blue eyes, and a big smile. She had brown curly shoulder-length hair, but usually pulled back in a ponytail. She sometimes wore makeup; the inmates would use coffee grounds for mascara and colored pencils for eyeliner. They also had a way of making things from food bought at the commissary. They would have top ramon and would add things to it and call it casserole. It was their ways of adapting to losing the simple things in life that we take for granted. Jessica had a way about her, as if she really thought about things, and she walked with a bold confidence. She seemed young and determined to learn from her lessons and do something different with her life. Later, after getting to know more about her story, she told me she had been in and out of jail since she was eighteen. This time she knew she might go to prison. When she came to the studies, she told me that she never really knew much about God, but figured she would give it a try. Jessica had two kids, and she said that she wanted her kids back and her life back, and now she wanted God to be a part of it. She said, "I want to break this cycle I've been in." She was determined that this time, the revolving door was going to stop!

Never in my wildest dreams did I think my work would benefit anyone to the extent that it did. You know, as you give out, it does something to your soul, too; it lifts you up. Finally, Jessica left to go to Purdy, which was the state prison. I would get sweet letters and cards from her explaining what she was doing with her time. She was cooking, reading, and taking classes, but mostly deciding how things would be different once she left. I believe she was in there for longer than a year. I would write her back, and finally, I decided I would venture out to Purdy to visit her.

My friends and I drove over to an area where the prison was located. We spent the night at her sister's home. They were nice enough to let me borrow their vehicle for a few hours, so I could go over and meet with Jessica. I drove for miles to a facility that was located in the sticks. There were no buildings around or neighborhoods close by. There were multiple signs on the road that said: Don't pick up hitchhikers, as well as signs posting huge fines for picking up inmates.

I got to the facility, checked in, and they took me over to the cafeteria. Jessica had no idea I was coming. I was waiting patiently by the vending machines when I saw her walk in. She was so happy and surprised to see me, she looked like she was being given a birthday cake lit up with candles.

She said, "Ginny, I can't believe you came! You are the only person who has come to see me! Not even my own family has come to see me!" She was blown away.

I told Jessica, "I wanted to do this. I feel you have something to offer others, and you are special and I care about you."

She kept saying, "I can't believe you came to see me."

I forget these special moments at times, but these are the kind of things that kept me doing what I was doing. We ended up eating food from the vending machines and talked about her kids, and what she would do when she was out of prison. Her plan was to go to a clean house and then get a job, and eventually get her kids back.

We talked about spiritual things and she said she was keeping up on the devotions, but it was pretty personal and private to her. Finally, she had to leave and she said, "I'll see you on this date." We were counting the days until she returned! We were both excited for her to get out.

It finally happened. She got into a clean and sober home and then found a job. Eventually, she got her kids back and the relationship between her and her mom was restored. A restored life. It was a miracle, and with God's help, she did a lot of her own work. We started having church gatherings in the home that she and her mom were renting, and she would invite friends that she felt would be open to God and his spirit's leading. It wasn't anything like

mainstream Christian churches. I felt God's power and presence was important to have available to do the greater things that the church was supposed to do.

Jessica's little son Colby, who was about nine years old, decided to make a commitment to Christ and his ways, and he and Jessica decided that they both wanted to be baptized. I thought, *Where in the heck do I get a baptismal for these two?* I spoke to a lady from my church whose daughter was in to a spiritual group called "The Broken Chains." I spoke to the minister from that group; he had been a street kid himself and had a real vision to help the street kids.

He said he could do the baptism, so Colby, Jessica, and another young woman decided to go ahead with it.

It was a wonderful to be part of this process. She kept saying, "Ginny, I want you to baptize me." I said, "I can't, this isn't my church, but I am here beside you, so please just be ok with that." She and her son both got up explained how they had wanted God in their lives, and how it had affected their family. Their faces were radiant from being baptized. Jessica and I are still in contact to this day. I have a deep caring for her. I hope and pray that Christ still lives in their hearts and they listen to his spirit.

Now, as time goes on, I have gone from leading studies to becoming a chaplain at the work center. When I was invited to become a chaplain, I thought, *No way! No schooling? No certificates?* I thought you had to go to school or get special training to do that. They told me to just walk and observe a few people who were chaplains. I thought, *Well, I guess the disciples that Christ walked with didn't go to college.* They learned by the spirit and were connected; they learned and were taught by that.

It's been a great opportunity and what a wonderful blessing it has been. I spoke to a lady who was doing a two-year study and others who did internships. And I was able to just walk right in. God was surely leading me! Another synchronicity and miracle!

In being a chaplain, I have heard many a story and seen many a tear; I have helped to heal many things and bring deep secrets out of the souls of women to feel cleansed of them. I've seen drug addicts, prostitutes, women who have deep pain from being abused sexually and emotionally, and helped them to realize that God loves them and can heal their pain. Just the other day, I prayed for someone who said to me, "Please pray for me. I'm nuts!" And I said, "Sure, I'll pray," and God came through and she felt his goodness and peace towards her.

Many of these folks have deep regrets, but all we have is NOW— we can't change the past. We just have to live in the now, and for the future we will have. If you feel you need to let go of the past and want to move on, you can! Sometimes people just don't know where to start.

CHAPTER 6 - SPIRITUAL WISDOM

Sometimes we have to pause to observe and
listen to the wisdom!

Nature's wisdom reflects God's wisdom. This is because nature is a part of God. Look at the animal kingdom. Animals go with the cycles of life. Migration during winter and then nesting and shedding skins or building nests to keep warm. They accept without questioning the system of the earth and its cycles, they just go with the flow of life. They go with the cycles of the morning sun and the rhythms of the moon and flow with the changing seasons.

We can learn from animals and nature and what they give us. Many say, Oh, it's just an animal. But look at the animals. The animals take care of their offspring, and many times they will take care of other animals which aren't their own species. Sometimes animals stay in packs to protect what they have and support one another and get the food they need.

Sometimes animals will care about a young one that doesn't even belong to them. I've seen kittens that have been abandoned and a dog will nurse it, or care for it as its own. Now that is a miracle. Sometimes, people will do that when they adopt, but often people's attitudes are, I am not responsible for that person, so I am not going to worry about it. We are all connected and must feel for others, including the animals.

Look at the birds, the fish, the bears — they know they are taken care of and may look for food, but they don't seem to worry. The world just takes care of them. Didn't God say in the Bible not to worry, as he takes care of the birds of the air? We can learn from animals. We should take care of them. We must leave room for nature and for the natural evolution of things on the earth. We must listen to how the cycles of life tell us things.

We can learn from the animals and how they support one another and help each other in a community. Living in the community comes with its benefits. Many animal species instinctively know to stick together. Do they experience compassion and empathy? It is well established that elephants mourn their dead.

Why do you think God told us to care for the animals and take care of what was given to mankind? We need to care for Mother

Nature as well as the people inhabiting the earth. We have destroyed the earth with our consumption and by not taking loving care of what we have been given. If we continue on this planet, we must love all the creatures on the planet. Otherwise, we will go extinct. We have to start thinking what we need, and realizing how it affects the whole of God's creation. We have to take care of nature as it takes care of us.

We can learn spiritual lessons from some of the folk wisdom about animals handed down from our ancestors.

Wise as an Owl

Once I was in a church sanctuary where the congregation was having an auction to earn money. There were some beautiful photographs of snowy owls taken by a photographer who went up to British Columbia for three-weeks. These great creatures came and communed there for that short period of time. It made me think about the expression "wise as an owl." The eyes in the photos pierced my soul; I could see the depth in them. The snowy owl is considered especially wise.

Why is an owl considered wise? I read about the owl and learned he has huge eyes and can see in the night time. They use wisdom to survive and get their prey, just like we have to be wise and see things as they are. The owl's head rotates all around so he can see his prey. God made him that way, but he knows how to use his talents to best benefit the life he has been given. Also, a wise owl knows when best to take his prey and sometimes we have to do that. Know our talents, and use our talents appropriately. See when it is the best time to do something. Sometimes we have to wait, other times we lunge forward. We must have spiritual eyes to see, just like the owl; it knows.

God knows what the best time is, and we need to praise him all the time. Is it easy to do? It's not always easy because we don't understand, but God does have a plan. You see, the birds and the fish just go with the flow and don't try to make things happen, as they trust the currents of wind and water and the cycles of life. Sometimes we strive too hard and that is not the way. It's going with the flow of life and seeing the traps like animals do, so they can achieve what they are supposed to.

Busy as a Bee

Bees work very hard and they are born with a purpose. There are worker bees, drones made for mating, and a queen in a hive. To fulfill that purpose they work together, and work very hard and are busy completing the task that is set before them. They all know their role. They don't go beyond that role, they see that role, sharpen that role, keep their focus on what their job is. It's the same with us. We must complete the task that is set before us to establish a kingdom. A new kingdom here on earth. We must love our assignment and complete it.

Strong as an Ox

Oxen are strong and powerful, and so must we be. We have to be strong and powerful in what we feel is before us. We have to withstand what is before us which could prevent us from getting where we need to be. We have to stay close to the source to stay strong. Oxen or animals typically do work with yokes upon them. When working together they are stronger when pulling the weight with the yokes. If they don't work together, it cannot be as effective. As Christ said, "my burden is easy and the yoke is light." This load shouldn't be hard but light as we have someone working with us.

Sly as a Fox

Foxes are clever and smart. We must use all our facilities and judgments to be clever and smart to accomplish our spiritual goals and purposes in life. We must see when we could potentially be trapped, and how we could potentially get detoured from our life purpose and could steal from us if we are to achieve our destiny and spiritual path.

Another aspect of the fox is they are quick to move when hunting their prey, which makes them known as being swift and quick to act. That teaches us that sometimes we have to do the same, be quick to action and swift. Sometimes foxes romp and play in the snow; this can teach us to take opportunities to play and enjoy the moment and live enthusiastically.

CHAPTER 7 - MIRACLES HAPPEN TO THOSE WHO BELIEVE

You are the miracle and you have to trust that God has a plan. Just like the birds, the fish, and the rivers and streams trust life. We are the miracle of life and sometimes we take it for granted. Life is a miracle and there is something bigger and greater directing our lives.

I want to share some stories about God working in the everyday lives of people whose lives were touched by something greater than themselves.

Miracle 1. Somebody I knew named Steve was distraught and thinking that his life wasn't worth living. He took his motorcycle for a ride and decided that day he would take his life. He was driving along and looking for a way for it would happen. He saw a big semi-truck, and just as he was about to turn his motorcycle into the truck, a warmth went through his whole body and a voice out of nowhere said, " No, I have a different plan." You see, God had a different plan and his plan was to restore Steve's life. Steve was discouraged. He didn't have hope. He was tired and there were some unfortunate things that had happened to him, but he listened to the voice. Steve started taking control of his life: filling his mind with good thoughts, eating well, and before he knew it, things started turning around. God sees all and knows all. Steve was a miracle waiting to happen!

God knows the intentions of our hearts, and what we are going through. Even in the darkest of times, God has the power, and may send his angels or things to minister to us to show us the way. Sometimes, we may be the angel for a person in need to speak life into their very own soul. That day Steve had a choice—a choice to stay on that motorcycle and make the turn, but he didn't. He decided to listen to the voice. Steve took the way that leads to life. Don't take the path that leads to death, but take LIFE. Choose this day life or death. You see, God knew Steve's life and knew what he needed. Choose this day!

Miracle 2. I was driving one day and there was a man in a wheelchair. My heart went out to him when I saw him in his motorized wheelchair. Something in my spirit said, "Go find him." We have to listen to those inner promptings. So I did! I drove back and kept looking for the man in my rearview mirror. It was dark. I finally parked my car and went running down the streets looking for the wheelchair. There it is, I said to myself. I quickly found him. As I stood there, I really didn't know what to say, but I told him I just was checking on him, and I asked if he had a faith. He said, "Yes," and "It's been a very hard day." That day I gave someone hope.

I asked him if I could pray with him and he said, "I would love that." I thanked God for our interaction and felt like it really helped him. I could sense the hope in his heart. I was blessed in that I was being used to help encourage this man. It was a small act, but small acts can change a person's life in ways only God knows. We have to listen to the spirits working in us to show those who need encouragement.

Miracle 3. Another time, I was driving on the road one night after work. It was a cold night and it was dark. I saw a man crossing the street and he looked like he was limping, and like he was hurting. My heart told me I wanted to go out to help him. Right at that moment, a surge of energy went shooting quickly down my right leg. I felt that was my sign to turn around. (One of my friends later kidded me, "Are you sure that wasn't a sign that you should have stepped on the gas and gone home." I laughed, but I was glad I didn't.) I drove around and looked for the man and saw him walking through a parking lot, so I pulled into the mall and made a few more turns and then found him. As I approached him, I saw that he had brown hair, a beard, and a baseball cap and was holding a small white and brown dog. I thought, *I really should stay in my car to protect myself.* Even though my intuition told me to stop, I still needed to be wise.

I motioned to the man and said, "Sir, can you please come over?"

He did and I thought, *What the heck do I say now? God didn't give me any words to actually say to him.* I said, "My name is Ginny, and I feel God has shown me to come and talk to you. You must be pretty special."

He said, "Ma'am, this is the best news I've heard all day today. You have no idea what I have been through this last year. I lost my home because I was diagnosed with cancer and wasn't able to cover the mortgage, so I am homeless. Also, my mom passed away just last week." Then he said, "It's been pretty challenging, to be honest."

I said, "Well you know God must have known you needed some encouragement. So, here I am, can we pray?" So we prayed and I asked God to encourage him and I also prayed for his healing.

As we finished, he said with a tear in his eye, "Thank you very much. You don't know how much this has touched me. Thank you and bless you."

I told him, "You don't need to thank me, thank God and have gratitude that he sees and knows all that you have gone through."

He looked at me again and said, "I have a deep love for my Father and this has uplifted my spirit."

Sometimes, God sends those to speak life to our spirits. God sees everything and we have to be open to those signs and take them.

Are you taking the signs? Sometimes, it can be awfully scary to listen to our gut and go with it, but if you don't, you may end up missing an opportunity to help another or even give words of hope. It can happen anywhere. You have to listen to that still small voice or even that loud voice that may be talking to you. There is a scripture that says: MY sheep hear my voice. Are you listening to that voice? Are you listening to the signs? I am glad I did because it blessed me, as much as it blessed him.

God can talk to us in the everyday occurrences. I was working out at a gym in my town. There was a Hispanic guy in his early twenties with a big afro, and he was pacing back and forth. I could see from afar that he was angry and anxious. I started praying for the man and thought to myself, What is his deal? and why is he so angry? You see, we have to look for opportunities and sometimes they will be made.

While I was on the treadmill working out, God told me to tell him that he loved him, and I thought, *I can't do that! I can't go up to a total stranger and tell him of a God who loved him.* I thought this was absolutely weird, and questioned what I had heard. I argued and questioned myself about what I had heard and thought there was no way I could do it. I went into the locker room and was about ready to leave the gym. I decided to leave without saying what I felt in my spirit that I was supposed to say to this man. I walked out of the building, but then turned around and decided I'd better do it. I thought to myself, *This guy is either going to be belligerent with me or accept what I say, or say, 'whatever lady!'*

I took the risk. I went up to him right there on the spot and said, "Hey, I don't know you, but I want to mention something to you." Then I gulped and said, "God loves you!"

He looked at me dumbfounded, and with a soft voice he said, "Thank you very much."

I looked at him and asked him his name and I said, "I will pray for you."

I surely did, every day for a while. About two weeks went by, and I went back to the gym. A man next to me on the treadmill said, "Hey, aren't you the lady who told my friend David that God loves him?" I said yes, and then he began to tell me that his friend had actually stepped into a church. I spoke with him that day. It just so happened that he hadn't been in one in five years, and it really spoke to his heart and affirmed to him up that God really loved him. He said, "You know I've been praying for him, for a while now. He is from New York and has a bad temper, and has a lot of anger, please pray for him."

I told him I would continue. God knew that, but I didn't know his situation. Wow, it really was ordained to speak to him, I thought to myself. *I am so glad I did what I was supposed to.*

A few days passed and his friend, who is a Muslim, came up to me and said, "Hey, are you the lady that God speaks to?"

I said, "Yes!"

He said, "You know I go to temple up in Canada and really want to know God. I follow all the rules and try to do the right thing. I try to live morally, but I don't have a relationship with him like you do."

I said, "Do you want to come to church with me? You can have a relationship with him. Do you want to have a relationship where you can hear God for yourself? You can, you know."

Then, he asked me to please pray for him and a girl that he really loved. He was supposed to come to church with me, but we could never connect. I hope and pray that he found his path. Sometimes saying the words God tells you can have a boomerang effect, and you don't know by saying one simple word, how it can change a multitude of people.

God is Speaking. Are We Listening?

God wants to speak to us in all kinds of ways. At the end of days, the Lord says he will give people dreams and visions. Sometimes dreams can give us warnings and give a bigger message. Have you had a dream where God is telling you something? Here is an inspiring true story by Jay L. Johnson that shares a message about the importance of listening to God when signs appear in your dreams.

The Ignored Call © 2005

I thought yesterday would be my last writing of 2016. But last night when I woke up again, I dreamed the same dream, and it's still pressing in heavy on me. Dreams are not strange to me. From the time I was a girl, I dreamed, many of them coming true. At that time while I was playin' church they scared me. I asked the Lord to stop them. Now I know they are a blessing. I have learned through the years when dreams plague me, I must act on them. They often affect either mine or someone else's life.

I've always told people I could run for office and not fear what the opposition may find out about me, I tell it all. Why? I am a voice of what many people go through and cannot tell themselves. I am the voice that says this happened and this is what God did, and this is How I've been changed, and where I am now because of God's Grace.

It was November 22, 1963, my last day at work at Montgomery Ward. I was leaving home for the first time to live with relatives I'd never met before. I was an adult, and I was free. I was so excited. Nothing could stop me from going to Kansas City, Mo. When I came home from work and turned on the TV I learned President Kennedy had been shot, later I heard he was killed. This was unheard of in the United States. This was beyond ugly, just like the dreams I had been having lately. Maybe that's what the dreams were trying to alert me to. Maybe my own dreams were foretelling of something like this really happening. Wow, this was powerful. I, like so many million who were in shock, cried, and mourned.

Several months before when I first started planning to go to Kansas City, I was lying in bed. My mom and I lived together in a large, three-room apartment. The bedroom was connected to the living room by French doors. Mom was in the living room watching TV. As I lay there almost sleeping, I heard my name. She knew I had to go to work early in the morning, why was she disturbing me; so, I answered "Mama?" She said, "What?" "Mama, you called me, what?" She replied that she hadn't, so I tried to go back to sleep.

The next time I wasn't sleeping, I heard my name again (spooky, right?), I thought, *she was playing a game with me, why I don't know.* But I got up out of bed and went into the living room. "Mama, I heard you say Jonita." Again, she said, "No I didn't." Then she said something that really scared me. "Jonita, if you hear it again, answer yes Lord." I went back to bed, but I thought, *she had lost it.* And no matter what, I wasn't going to reply to something that wasn't there – she was crazy. Well, I did hear it again. I pulled the covers over my head and went to sleep. At 17 I wasn't going to pay any attention to voices coming out of nowhere (Didn't know about Samuel). With so much happening in my life, I put it out of my mind, but I never completely forgot it.

At some point before the assassination of President Kennedy, I started having dreams. The same dream EVERY night. Mama was scared for me and tried to talk me out of going to Kansas City, but I wouldn't hear of it. I was free, Black and almost grown at 18.

The Dream: I was getting on a Greyhound bus. Every seat was taken, and there was still one for me. I saw other young people of different races. There were old people and middle-aged people, most were smiling and ready to leave. The driver came on last, greeted everyone, and shut the doors. I pulled out a fashion magazine and was engrossed. When I looked up at the people around me, they had turned into animals; some farm, some wild. I was the only one who was normal. Even the driver had turned into a big hog. I was terrified. No one said anything to me, but they glared and watched my every move. The bus pulled into a farm for a stop, everyone turned into regular people right before my eyes. They got off, but I wasn't allowed to leave the bus. I tried to pry the doors open; they were locked, and the driver, who had turned into a pig in a uniform, stood outside holding the key and laughing. I woke up always in a sweat. This dream continued until I left on a train to Kansas City.

When I got there, I had nothing to fear, my family was great, respectable people. I found a job at a hospital and made friends with a beautiful girl my age. We worked, drank and partied hard together. It was my dream to be a model. So when I found an ad in the newspaper for models wanted, I answered it. My friend went with me, and we took great pictures. A week later they called me back and said, they needed one more girl for a shoot, would I come in. I did. I was paid big money for some slightly (okay, more than) indecent pictures. A week later, I was arrested and taken to jail. Being that I had just turned 18 one month before, I was tried as an adult. For months I had to go back and forth from Minnesota to KC for trial. I was so scared and promised God and Mama I'd never do anything so stupid, immoral or illegal. God intervened. Everyone with me had a previous record and served time, but me. It was the first offense.

Up until many years later, I didn't understand why God saved me. The dream was a warning of what was to come. I didn't want to hear Him speak to me while I was still at home and safe. I didn't listen to His voice calling my name to get my attention and lead me out of harm's way. God had tried to give me a warning, but I wanted what I wanted.

How often do we as Christian's ignore God's calls to us? God loves us so much and makes every attempt to lead and guide us to His perfect plan for our lives. Over the years, God has continued to help me through dreams. The lady Jay said my dreams are becoming more intense, more frequent. I have learned to listen. In my old age, I have learned to separate the voice of my Lord from other voices that call out for our attention. Folks the only way you can recognize His voice is to be in communication with Him; to be in an ongoing relationship with Him. Jesus is not a part-time Savior or a friend.

His Spirit is in us, resides in us as His Word is planted and grown in us.

You see, we have to be open—open to one leading us. Sometimes it's a strong urge. Other times it's a dream or a vision. Sometimes, something is shown to us. We have to be open. There is a big universe that has all kinds of ways that it speaks to us. This

universe which God created and God uses to direct our path can show us signs and wonders if we only listen to the cues. He did say these signs will accompany those who believe. Just like this woman who had a dream but really didn't know what it meant. It was trying to show her something. She wasn't sure what it was but she wasn't keeping her eyes wide open like the owls watching and waiting. We must watch and wait at times to see what is going on.

Once I met a woman who shared a story with me about a lesson she had learned about listening to divine guidance. This is what she told me.

God/Divine is a God of relationship to tell me things that I normally wouldn't know what the path is or what I am supposed to do next. God began to tell me while I was working at the beauty shop that he brought me to that it was time to go. There wasn't apparently anything wrong at the beauty shop. It actually was quite grand. I had been there for 9 years working at this facility where ladies came and got their hair done and I was serving them. I was making them feel beautiful and cared for. It seemed like a win/win situation. We all had such fun. I felt this leading and was a bit afraid and wasn't sure exactly what I was to do. I needed a way to support myself, but something in my spirit said it is time to go. I sensed it, but was afraid to step out.

A few days later the whole feeling was very heavy in my heart. They called me into the office of the management of the retirement home and I thought, *they were going to ask me to add another chair.* It was far from my mind to think anything would change because everyone was so happy there. They all seemed to love me. The day was over with and I was called in to talk to the boss, who said that they would like me to leave. I was like, leave what do you mean leave? Is everything ok? They said I wasn't consistent and would like someone who was more reliable. That didn't make any sense to me.

Then this woman remembered another time in her life when she had a big disappointment that didn't make any sense. But it dramatically changed her life. She decided to not fight the situation and just go with the flow and realized that something was changing and she was prepared for it as it was shown to her.

Later that day, she found out that one of the ladies whose hair she had done went to the management and reported that she was thinking of leaving. So that misinformation had gotten the woman fired. However, she had already been thinking about leaving her job, and so it wasn't completely false. Instead of fighting it, she decided to grab all her belongings and walk out. She felt God had gotten her that job and just she needed to let go and God would supply her needs again. While doing this she realized she had to let go of her pride and ego. Doing this made her a stronger person and made her transform into something else. You see, God has a plan and he prepared her for what was going to happen. She didn't want to go, but she felt she was supposed to.

Sometimes the path guides us to what is in the heart. The heart is where the true life is, the Tree of Life. The tree of life is the invisible, the sacred thing that God or the divine wills for you. Sometimes, we are trying to listen, but there are still subtler things to hear that point the way... not a huge loud voice but a subtle one

What do *you wish* for?

Chapter 8 - What Do You Wish for?

You see, my friend, we all have choices. We can either see the dandelion as a weed or use it to wish that something better is coming and blow the seeds! God is good and we have to look at the wishes, intentions, or prayers and see the power in them. We have to believe the miracles and wish upon the dandelions of our lives and convert them into something different. Make a wish, but also add dandelions to your diet... It may help!

BELIEVING IN YOURSELF

Are you looking to get closer to your spiritual destiny or purpose? We all have to believe in ourselves, but you also have to connect to something bigger than oneself. Prayer is a conversation. Prayer is when one goes to the depth of one's soul to understand the longing of one's true heart's desire. You commune with one whose intention is all love and whose love is unconditional. You go and commune and sense peace and love and through it, you will become a better person because you become the image of Christ. If you are a believer, no matter where the journey takes you, you will be strengthened in your inner purpose and become greater than yourself and evolve into a better HUMAN BEING.

Norman Vincent Peale once said, "Prayer begins where human capacity ends. They are impressive utterances of the heart that spur and change you to do something different in this world." You have to commune with your creator and connect. God is everything and everywhere—it's important to remember that.

We have to believe in ourselves that we all have talents and gifts that are special that only we can do. You have to believe that something is greater than yourself. That this force who created the whole world/universe has a plan. With this plan, there are secrets that need to be revealed and there are great mysteries through the ages that speak of wisdom and knowledge. Do we listen to these ancestors and the knowledge that they tell us? These gifts and talents are given to us to help each other. More so, to do the will of what God has sent us here on the planet to do. Having God in our lives gives us a greater capacity to love, to feel, and to be loved, more than what this world system tells us to be. By knowing God, we have a greater capacity to be loved and shown the way!

What sometimes stops us in our unbelief and our past— Is it fear? doubt? Only you may actually know. The ride isn't over yet, and we continue on!

Keep believing that you are the miracle. Sometimes the small miracles are like small kisses on our face while we are waiting for the bigger ones.

Believe that you can fly!

It's important to remember that. Sometimes it's just being thankful and being grateful for what we do have and seeing the hand of God in your life. Being thankful for the little things as well as the big things in life, such as the air we breathe, and having one's health.

Chapter 9 - Transformation

S ometimes we have a premonition that something is about to change. We don't like change, but change is necessary for transformation. Something in my spirit kept saying it's a BIRTH-day, it was whispering, but something new was happening. I kept seeing butterflies all over the place, which means transformation. I decided to go with it. Butterflies symbolize the resurrection of Christ in which something more powerful and beautiful is emerging. Butterflies can also symbolize the wonder of Life and Spiritual Transformation, being reborn into an entirely new way of being. Butterflies are graceful and go from one flower to the next. They emerge from a cocoon into a beautiful new thing!

Butterflies are magical, and that is how we should view life! Caterpillars are eating machines and they are very self-focused and grow instantly. Sometimes caterpillars can cause much damage and cause health issues and disease. We can't stay in this caterpillar stage where we are only self-focused and cause damage, but we go into the cocoon stage and emerge from our old self to become that something new. We become the power through deep reflection and become our greater self. All is possible and the butterfly represents that power, joy, love, elegance, and beauty. We will see what is next? Sometimes it's hard to make changes, but with these changes sometimes with the transplanting, the roots grow stronger and deeper.

Sometimes, we have to stop striving and allow the process. Stop looking at the future and realize that in being, we are the house, the house that is the strong foundation for something to become. Sometimes the transformation can become the miracle. We have to believe we are the miracle. The miracle that we live and breathe— knowing that something bigger than ourselves made us. When we believe we are a miracle, we start acting like a miracle, and we are divinely guided. We act the way we are intended to be and realize the good that surrounds us.

Christ worked Miracles. Aside from us being the miracle, we also were made able to do miracles. Christ healed the sick, raised the dead, and cast out the leper, and so shall we. We have a power inside of us to be able to vibrate at the higher energy of love and well-being so that we can change the atmosphere around us. Is it easy to be the miracle? We have to consciously take on a new mindset, the mind of Christ, and be transformed to be a miracle to do the greater things! True love is giving. God gave his son so that we would learn to give, and on it goes. Being the light is giving, producing something bigger than ourselves.

You Are the Miracle!

What does the word "miracle" actually mean? Webster's dictionary defines it as "an amazing or wonderful occurrence." The noun comes from the Latin *miraculum,* "object of wonder." Dig way back and the word derives from *smeiros*, meaning "to smile," which is exactly what you do when a miracle happens! A miracle is something amazing—Do you realize you are amazing?

Being a miracle means you have something special in this world to give. You were made with a plan and a purpose but you have to listen to the WAY. Christ and the disciples did miracles, and miracles are commanded by our voice and what we speak. That is why it is so important to speak life and to speak the way and vibrate that truth.

Today when you speak blessings or curses, we have the power in our tongues and we vibrate truth. There were many things people spoke that allowed miracles with the water: the red sea was parted; Elijah pronounced drought upon the land and it lasted for three years; Christ changed water into wine. There was a multiplication of food to feed five thousand, and at Christ's word, the dead came back from life. Aren't we supposed to be the miracle to be able to do greater things in his name? But we have to take on the character and the image and be transformed!

Life is a miracle and so many of us take our life for granted. We have to live life on our own terms instead of how society is telling us to live. We all get caught up in how everybody is doing things or living their lives. We get programmed into thinking this is how we should live. Be authentic and live within a spiritual force that is guiding you and showing the way. We have to believe there is a bigger purpose, a grander plan than what we have in mind. How could we just come here for no purpose? There is a big universe that is breathing and living for our ultimate good. Why don't we see each other as miracles and be kind to each other? We have a whole big world where we could be working together for the good of everyone, for the good of humanity.

What Do You Want?

This last section is a time of reflection on it is what do you truly want.

Do you want peace?

Do you want hope?

Do you want fulfillment?

The questions in this section of the book will, I hpe, inspire you to see something grander for your life.

Become something beautiful.

1. What is your passion? Are you living it?

_____

_____

_____

_____

_____

2. Are you a game changer or are you stuck in a rut?

_____

_____

_____

_____

_____

3. Do you question what your purpose is for being on this earth?
   Or are you living on purpose? When are you at your best?

_____

_____

_____

_____

_____

4.Do you feel something nudging you to make a change? If so, what is that? Is there something you are waiting to explore?

_____

_____

_____

_____

_____

5.Do you follow the crowd? If so, why? What would it feel like to get out of the box?

_____

_____

_____

_____

_____

6.Is there something you've been told you're good at since you were a child? Are you doing this now? If not, why not?

_____

_____

_____

_____

_____

7.Is there something you are being shown to do? What are the signs?

_____

_____

_____

_____

_____

8.Are you open to new things? If so, what would that be? What do you need to let go of?

_____

_____

_____

_____

_____

9.Is there a lesson you have to learn and master before going forward?

_____

_____

_____

_____

_____

10. If you could create your life, what would it be like? What do you most desire?

_____

_____

_____

_____

_____

11. .If you were to write out step-by-step goals to your vision, how would you set things up to make it happen?

_____

_____

_____

_____

_____

12. Are you happy with how things are in your life? If not, why not? How would you want things to be different?

_____

_____

_____

_____

_____

13.Do you view life as having exciting possibilities? What are
they?

_____

_____

_____

_____

_____

Acknowledgements

I want to thank the people in my life - my parents who taught me to love God, and placed that in my heart as a young child; my spiritual mentors who spoke life into me, as well as family/friends, and other authors, who encouraged me to write this book.

I am thankful for my book team:

I am grateful to my editor Kendra Langeteig, who believed in me and guided me through the book writing journey. I am grateful to artist Barry Donaldson, for the beautiful painting to illustrate the cover of my book. I am grateful to Aubree Jensen for her eye for graphic design and the flair she added to my work. For Norman L Green, the typesetter, and the creative way he took the book with his design

More information on these people

Aubree Jensen is a graphic designer in Northwest Washington. Along with working full time, she loves opportunities to freelance on the side. You can view her portfolio at aubreejdesign.com.

Barry Donaldson is a Visionary artist currently living in the hills of Tennessee. His artwork merges the beauty of nature with mystic qualities of the spiritual realm. It has also been known to touch hearts and intrigue minds while ushering in sense of harmony and understanding in these often tumultuous times.

www.ArtistofEden.com

Norman L Green of Threshold Documents, Bellingham, Washington. www.ThresholdDocuments.com

Kendra Laneteig is a book doctor and publishing consultant at Edgewise Publishing in Bellingham, Washington.

77872646R00071

Made in the USA
San Bernardino, CA
29 May 2018